100
Best
Gluten-Free

100
Best
Gluten-Free

Your guide to gluten-free eating including 100 delicious recipes

This edition published by Parragon Books Ltd in 2014 and distributed by

Parragon Inc.
440 Park Avenue South, 13th Floor
New York, NY 10016
www.parragon.com/lovefood

LOVE FOOD is an imprint of Parragon Books Ltd

ISBN 978-1-4723-5469-3

Printed in China

Created and produced by made-to-measure-books
New photography by Clive Streeter
Nutritional consultant: Judith Wills

Nutritional data obtained from the USDA national nutrient database.

Notes for the Reader

This book uses standard kitchen measuring spoons and cups. All spoon and cup measurements are level unless otherwise indicated. Unless otherwise stated, milk is assumed to be whole, eggs are large, individual vegetables are medium, and pepper is freshly ground black pepper. Unless otherwise stated, all root vegetables should be peeled prior to using.

Garnishes, decorations, and serving suggestions are all optional and not necessarily included in the recipe ingredients or method. The times given are only an approximate guide. Preparation times differ according to the techniques used by different people and the cooking times may also vary from those given. Optional ingredients, variations, or serving suggestions have not been included in the time calculations.

While the author has made all reasonable efforts to ensure that the information contained in this book is accurate and up to date at the time of publication, anyone reading this book should note the following important points:

Medical and pharmaceutical knowledge is constantly changing and the author and the publisher cannot and do not guarantee the accuracy or appropriateness of the contents of this book.

In any event, this book is not intended to be, and should not be relied upon, as a substitute for appropriate, tailored professional advice. Both the author and the publisher strongly recommend that a healthcare practitioner is consulted before making major dietary changes.

For the reasons set out above, and to the fullest extent permitted by law, the author and publisher: (i) cannot and do not accept any legal duty of care or responsibility in relation to the accuracy or appropriateness of the contents of this book, even where expressed as "advice" or using other words to this effect; and (ii) disclaim any liability, loss, damage, or risk that may be claimed or incurred as a consequence—directly or indirectly—of the use and/or application of any of the contents of this book.

CONTENTS

INTRODUCTION

Celiac disease—an autoimmune disease that causes the body to produce antibodies to react to gluten—affects around 1 in 100 people throughout the world. The only cure is to avoid gluten completely. For life. Gluten is one of the proteins found in wheat, barley, and rye, and it is also in many processed foods, but, thankfully, there is no need to feel deprived when you are on a gluten-free diet. With a little know-how, you can have a varied, nutritionally balanced, and enjoyable diet.

Celiac disease damages the small intestine and can result in unpleasant symptoms, such as nausea, bloating/gas, diarrhea, and constipation, which can be debilitating. The resulting damage to the intestine causes malabsorption of nutrients, leading to other symptoms, such as tiredness, headaches, canker sores, hair loss, anemia, osteoporosis, and weight loss, so it is important that it is properly diagnosed. Anyone recently diagnosed with celiac disease needs as nutritious and beneficial a diet as possible, because they may have been experiencing poor nutrient absorption for some time.

Some people who don't have celiac disease also follow a gluten-free diet, and the number of those who want to cut gluten from their diet is increasing. These people may experience bloating, gas, indigestion, and irritable bowel syndrome, for example, and feel a gluten-free diet helps minimize these symptoms. Or it may

be a personal choice, because they may simply feel more healthy on a gluten-free diet.

As well as being in wheat, barley, and rye, gluten is also found in many processed foods that contain small amounts of these grains and their by-products. Some people are also sensitive to avenin, a protein similar to gluten found in oats. Many oats may also be contaminated with gluten because they are packaged in the same factories as wheat, barley, or rye, so most celiacs avoid oats, too. Look for oats labeled as gluten-free if you still want to include them in your diet.

Foods to avoid on a gluten-free diet

The most obvious foods that may contain gluten are those that normally contain wheat, such as breads, crackers, breakfast cereals, pasta, flour, pastry, cakes, and cookies. Many other foods contain wheat, rye, or barley in smaller amounts; for example, breaded and battered fish and nuggets, beverages such as beer, desserts, confectionery, packaged and canned soups and stocks. This isn't a comprehensive list. For more information, contact a support organization (such as Celiac.com) for details of foods that contain gluten and those that are gluten-free, as well as to learn about new gluten-free labeling information.

Food choices on a gluten-free diet

There are many choices of grains and "pseudo grains" that do not contain gluten and many of these, such as quinoa, teff, amaranth, rice, and buckwheat, are actually richer in health-protecting and health-promoting nutrients.

As well as these great gluten-free grains, there is also a wide choice of other naturally gluten-free foods to provide carbs in your diet. Legumes (beans, lentils, and split peas) are rich in starch and come with higher levels of many of the vitamins and minerals, too. Several vegetables are high-carb—for example, sweet potatoes, parsnips, and beets—and these offer additional health benefits because most are rich in phytochemicals. Research into these plant chemicals shows that they are important in helping to prevent our most prevalent diseases and many health problems associated with aging. Other vegetables and some fruits are useful sources of carbohydrates, so there is plenty of choice.

There is much benefit in choosing a diet that is basically natural instead of highly processed. The natural foods highlighted in this book don't come with long ingredients lists that you need to check for gluten, and are probably more nutritious. However, supermarkets are stocking more and more ingredients and processed foods that are gluten-free items. Gluten-free pastas, breads, crackers, and cereals can add variety and convenience to your diet.

Get plenty of vitamins and minerals

There are several key nutrients that people following a gluten-free diet often lack: Vitamins A, B_1, B_2, niacin, folate, B_{12}, D, E, and K and the minerals calcium, iron, magnesium, phosphorous, and zinc.

By choosing a wide range of foods from this book to eat regularly, you will almost certainly get your recommended daily allowances of vitamins and minerals, as well as all the other nutrients and compounds we need for health. For example, a mix of gluten-free grains and legumes will provide carbs, protein, folate, and magnesium in abundance; fruit and vegetables are packed with phytochemicals, potassium, and vitamin C and leafy greens are rich in vitamin K. Nuts and seeds are rich in unsaturated fats and zinc, while meat provides high-quality protein, iron, phosphorous, and the B vitamins. From eggs we get vitamins A, D, and E; from fish and shellfish selenium and omega-3 fats; and from yogurt and cheese, calcium. And, of course, all these foods contain many other nutrients, too.

Using this book

Within these pages you will find detailed advice about which foods to choose to boost your intake of any particular nutrient. When a food is a particularly good source of that nutrient, we've highlighted it and you'll also find a list of the major nutrients that each food contains.

We have paid particular attention to foods that help promote digestive health. Some, such as cannellini beans, bananas, and pears, are particularly suitable for a sensitive digestive tract and can help reduce bloating, improve the digestive tract flora and help with conditions such as irritable bowel syndrome. Many foods here also offer protection against colon and bowel cancers.

We've come up with 100 great gluten-free recipes and ideas here for how to use our top 100 foods, but we are all individuals, all different, and there is no one diet that is the "perfect" diet. As long as you get a good variety and range of foods, simply choose the foods you enjoy.

Healthy eating tips

Here are a few healthy eating tips that will help you get the best out of your gluten-free diet.

• Try to eat at least five portions a day of vegetables and fruit. (Starchy root vegetables, such as potatoes, don't count.) Try to have at least one portion a day of a leafy green vegetable and one of mixed salad.

• Aim to have at least as many vegetable portions a day as you do fruit (don't have all your five just as fruit).

• Choose a selection of different-colored fruits and vegetables to make sure you get a wide selection of plant chemicals.

• Try to eat around three servings of a carb-rich food (such as rice, corn, sweet potatoes, gluten-free bread) each day.

• Have around three servings a day of a high-protein food (such as lean meat, fish, shellfish, hard cheese, tofu, lentils, nuts, legumes, yogurt).

• Choose foods rich in healthy fats (such as olive oil, nuts, salmon, pumpkin seeds) every day.

• For digestive health—and more pleasure when eating—try to eat regularly, chew food thoroughly, and relax while you eat. Little and often may also be a good mantra.

GLOSSARY

ALA Alpha-linolenic acid, one of the essential fatty acids we need in small, regular amounts, because it can't be produced in the body, is one of the omega-3 group of polyunsaturated fats. ALA can be converted into DHA and EPA (see opposite) by our bodies.

Amino acids The 22 "building blocks" of protein, which are contained in many foods in varying combinations and amounts. Eight of these are essential (nine in kids) because they can't be made from other foodstuffs in the diet.

Anti-inflammatory Having the ability to reduce inflammation in the body. Many immune system disorders, including celiac disease, result in abnormal inflammation. Rheumatoid arthritis is an inflammatory disease, but heart disease, asthma, and other conditions may all have inflammation as a factor.

Antioxidants Substances, such as some vitamins and minerals and many phytochemicals, that protect the body against the effects of free radicals, toxins, and pollutants by helping to prevent oxidization in foods and in the body. Oxidization is believed to damage body cells and is linked with disease and aging.

Blood lipids Types of fats that can be found in the bloodstream, sometimes binding with proteins to make, for example, LDL and HDL (see opposite). High levels in the blood—or an imbalance in the types—can be a risk factor for cardiovascular and other diseases.

Cholesterol A fatty substance in many foods, such as meat, fish, and dairy produce, and also manufactured in the liver, cholesterol is essential to the body but may also be an important risk factor in cardiovascular disease. (Also see HDL and LDL.)

Complete protein A food that contains the eight essential amino acids in ideal amounts. Essential amino acids are vital to help maintain and build muscle, for cell maintenance and repair, and for many other body functions.

DHA and **EPA** Docosahexaenoic acid and eicosapentaenoic acid are both "long chain" omega-3 fatty acids found in only the fatty tissues in fish. They appear to help reduce the risk of cardiovascular disease and high blood pressure.

Fatty acids The components of the types of fat in our food; there are 25 fatty acid types, most of which can be made in the body. Two, the essential fatty acids linoleic acid (one of the omega-6 group) and alpha-linolenic acid (one of the omega-3 group), cannot and must be provided through diet.

Flavonoids A group of several thousand antioxidant compounds found in fruits, vegetables, and other plant foods.

Free radicals Highly reactive, unstable atoms or molecules in the body that are a normal by-product of metabolism but which may, in excess, be a trigger factor for disease and aging.

Glycemic index A system of ranking carbohydrate foods according to their effect on blood sugar levels. A rank of 100 is the highest—glucose (the pure form of sugar) is 100 and reaches the bloodstream quickly. People with insulin resistance and type-2 diabetes are advised to follow a low Glycemic Index (low GI) diet.

HDL High-density lipoproteins (a mixture of fatty cholesterol and proteins) travel through the blood, helping to remove harmful LDL cholesterol and keep arteries clear, reducing the risk of cardiovascular disease.

Homocysteine An amino acid produced by the body. High levels can damage the artery linings and make it hard for blood to clot properly, increasing the risk of heart disease and strokes.

Insoluble fiber Consisting mainly of cellulose, this type of dietary fiber is found in many plant foods—grains and vegetables are particularly good sources. It helps to keep the digestive system working properly with regular bowel movements.

Insulin A hormone produced in the pancreas that controls the amount of glucose in the blood and helps the body use it for energy. People with type-2 diabetes (the most common type) may not produce enough insulin or may be resistant to the hormone.

LDL Low-density lipoproteins are microscopic particles of protein that transport cholesterol in the blood. High levels are linked with the formation of plaques, narrowing of the arteries, and coronary artery disease.

Phytochemicals Chemicals and compounds found in foods that can have many positive effects on health and disease prevention. Vegetables, fruits, grains, and legumes are our major sources.

Polyphenols A group of antioxidant plant chemicals found in many plant foods, with a proven effect in reducing the risk of some cancers and heart disease.

Prebiotics Indigestible carbohydrates, found in certain foods, such as onions and asparagus, that help promote the growth of "friendly" bacteria in the digestive tract.

Probiotics These are "friendly" bacteria, such as *acidophilus* and *bifidobacteria*, found in certain foods, such as yogurt with live cultures and miso, that help boost the immune system and have other health benefits.

Pseudo grains Starchy carbohydrate foods that are usually classified within the grain group of foods but are not true grains—they may be a fruit (such as buckwheat) or a seed (such as quinoa).

Soluble fiber A type of dietary fiber that, with water, turns to gel during digestion and helps slow down the rate at which it travels through the digestive tract. It may help ease digestive disorders and lower cholesterol. Some grains, nuts, seeds, and some fruits are particularly good sources.

Trans fats Most trans fats have been hardened from oils into solid fats in a process called hydrogenation, and they have been much used in mass food production. They raise LDL and lower HDL cholesterol. Some foods, such as lamb and regular dairy products, contain small amounts of trans fats naturally.

1

Grains and flours

A gluten-free diet doesn't mean that you need to be deprived
of healthy and versatile grains. Although some of the most
commonly used grains in the United States do contain
gluten, there is a good range of grains and pseudo grains
that can replace them perfectly. Most are nutritionally
superior as well—many are rich in high-quality protein,
as well as carbohydrate, and contain an excellent range of
minerals and health-protecting plant chemicals.

(C) High in carbohydrate

(F) Good source of fiber

(V) Rich in vitamins and minerals

(D) Particularly good for digestive health

(P) High in protein

(N) Nutrient boost for gluten-free diet

01

AMARANTH

These tiny seeds are high in protein and carbohydrate and rich in a wide range of vitamins and minerals.

Along with quinoa, amaranth seeds are one of the few plant foods to contain all the essential amino acids in a good balance, making them a valuable source of high-quality protein and a useful grain substitute for gluten-free eating. Their generous B-vitamin and mineral content increases their nutritional value. They are high in oxygen-transporting iron—a ⅓-cup/2¼-ounce portion will give you one-third of your RDA—and contain half your RDA of magnesium, which boosts heart and bone health. Studies have shown amaranth has a powerful cholesterol-lowering effect and the choline in the seeds is known to remove harmful homocysteine (associated with heart disease) from the blood.

- A good source of high-quality protein.
- High carbohydrate content ideal for the gluten-free diet.
- Rich in several of the B vitamins, including choline.
- Lowers cholesterol.

Practical tips:
Cook seeds in 2½ times their weight of water for up to 30 minutes, or until the water is absorbed. Sprinkle the cooked grains into salads and on vegetables, stir into soup, or serve as a side dish. They also make a delicious porridge and can even be popped like corn. Add amaranth flour, which has a nutlike flavor, to a gluten-free mixed flour for breads, pancakes, and muffins.

DID YOU KNOW?

The leaves of the amaranth plant are eaten as a vegetable in Mexico and Central and South American countries, where it is native.

NUTRIENTS PER AVERAGE PORTION (⅓ cup/2¼ oz DRY WEIGHT) AMARANTH SEED

Calories	223
Protein	8 g
Fat	4.2 g
Carbohydrate	39 g
Fiber	4 g
Vitamin B$_5$	0.9 g
Vitamin B$_6$	0.3 g
Choline	42 mg
Folate	49 mcg
Calcium	95 mg
Iron	4.6 mg
Magnesium	149 mg
Phosphorous	334 mg
Potassium	305 mg
Selenium	11.2 mcg
Zinc	1.7 mg

Chile and amaranth cornbread

MAKES 1 LOAF (C) (V) (N)

2–3 fresh red chiles, or to taste
¾ cup amaranth flour
¾ cup gluten-free white flour mix
¾ cup coarse cornmeal
1 tablespoon gluten-free
    baking powder
1 teaspoon gluten-free
    baking soda
1½ teaspoons salt
¼ cup sugar
1 cup shredded cheddar cheese
3 eggs
1 cup buttermilk
5 tablespoons butter, melted
    and cooled slightly, plus extra
    for greasing
⅓ cup fresh or frozen corn
    kernels, thawed if frozen

Method

1 Preheat the oven to 400°F. Preheat the broiler. Grease a 9 x 5 x 3-inch loaf pan.

2 Place the chiles under the preheated broiler and cook, turning occasionally, for 5–7 minutes, until blackened all over. Remove the skins and seeds and finely chop the flesh.

3 Sift together the amaranth flour, white flour mix, cornmeal, baking powder, baking soda, and salt into a large bowl. Stir in the sugar and cheese.

4 Whisk the eggs with the buttermilk and melted butter until well blended.

5 Make a well in the center of the flour mixture and pour in the egg mixture. Combine with a fork, gradually drawing in the dry ingredients from the side.

6 Stir in the chiles and corn and spoon the batter into the prepared pan, leveling the surface. Bake in the preheated oven for 40–45 minutes, until a toothpick inserted into the center comes out clean.

7 Let cool in the pan for about 10 minutes, then turn out onto a wire rack and let cool completely.

02 BUCKWHEAT

One of the most nutrient-rich grains available, buckwheat has been linked with many health benefits. The nutty, rich taste lends itself to many uses.

Buckwheat isn't a true cereal, but it can be used in a similar way to wheat. Regular consumption can lower total cholesterol and LDL cholesterol, and it can improve blood flow to the heart. This may be due to its high content of the blood-pressure lowering mineral potassium and its massive magnesium content (many gluten-free diets are low in magnesium). Because of its relatively high fiber, and high-quality protein content, it's also a great grain for diabetics, lowering both insulin response and blood sugars.

- Rich in many heart and circulation-friendly vitamins, minerals, and plant compounds.
- Regular consumption lowers risk of diabetes and insulin resistance.
- Contains a high level of zinc, for a carbohydrate, which is important for a healthy immune system.
- A good source of vitamin B2 and niacin, both of which can be in short supply on a gluten-free diet.

Practical tips:
Cook buckwheat like rice to accompany casseroles; add to soups and stews; or cool and use in salads to boost the protein content. Buckwheat flour makes great pancakes for breakfast and is the traditional flour used in blinis and soba noodles. The flour is also good in cake and bread flours, while buckwheat flakes make a tasty addition to a homemade muesli or granola.

DID YOU KNOW?

Buckwheat is the fruit seed of a plant that is related to rhubarb and sorrel; it was widely cultivated in China more than 1,000 years ago.

NUTRIENTS PER AVERAGE PORTION (⅓ CUP/2¼ OZ DRY WEIGHT) BUCKWHEAT

Calories	206
Protein	7.9 g
Fat	2 g
Carbohydrate	42.9 g
Fiber	6 g
Vitamin B₂	0.26 mg
Vitamin B₅	0.7 g
Folate	18 mcg
Niacin	4.2 mg
Iron	1.3 mg
Magnesium	139 mg
Potassium	276 mg
Selenium	11.2 mcg
Zinc	1.4 mg

Golden pilaf

SERVES 4 (C) (F) (V) (N)

2 cups gluten-free vegetable or
    chicken stock
1¼ cups toasted buckwheat
3 tablespoons olive oil
1 onion, thinly sliced
2 garlic cloves, thinly sliced
¾-inch piece fresh ginger,
    thinly sliced
½ teaspoon ground turmeric
½ teaspoon ground cinnamon
¼ cup orange juice
½ cup golden raisins
2 carrots, coarsely grated
⅓ cup pine nuts, toasted
salt and pepper, to taste
fresh cilantro, to garnish

Method

1 Bring the stock to a boil in a large saucepan and add the
    buckwheat. Simmer for 5–6 minutes, until most of the liquid is
    absorbed, then add 1 tablespoon of the oil, cover, and let cook
    over low heat for 10 minutes, until tender.
2 Heat the remaining oil in a large skillet and sauté the onion over
    medium heat for 5–6 minutes, stirring occasionally, until soft and
    golden brown.
3 Add the garlic and ginger and stir for 1 minute, then stir in the
    turmeric, cinnamon, orange juice, and golden raisins and cook
    for 1 minute. Add the carrots, cooked buckwheat, and pine nuts,
    stirring until evenly heated. Season with salt and pepper.
4 Pile the pilaf onto a warm serving plate and garnish with cilantro.

03 CORN

One of the most popular starchy foods across the Western world, bright yellow and naturally sweet, corn is an ideal and adaptable cereal for any gluten-free diet.

Corn not only tastes good, it also contains a wide variety of antioxidant chemicals, including the carotenes lutein and zeaxanthin (vital for good vision) and other carotenes that our bodies convert to vitamin A, which is deficient in many people following a gluten-free diet. Another antioxidant in corn is coumarin for cancer prevention, a healthy vascular system, and lower blood pressure. Corn is a good source of choline, a member of the B-vitamin group (which helps to regulate fat metabolism, supports the liver, brain function, and nervous system, and is an anti-inflammatory) and also of vitamin B5 pantothenic acid, which helps release energy from sugars, starches, and fats.

• Rich in carotenes, including lutein and zeaxanthin, for eye health.
• Contains coumarin for cancer prevention and vascular health.
• High in potassium and antioxidants to control blood pressure.
• Fresh corn is a useful source of vitamin C.

Practical tips:
Eat fresh or frozen corn kernels or cobs for the highest levels of the B and C vitamins. Grits is a Southern dish made with cornmeal (dried and ground corn) boiled into a creamy porridge—ideal as a side dish for meat, chicken, or other main dishes. The Italian-style polenta is similar, and a quick-cooking version is available in larger supermarkets. Use coarse cornmeal to coat fish or chicken before baking or frying, or to make cornbread or corn fritters. Cornstarch, which is generally used as a thickener for sauces or as a bulking agent, has little nutritional value.

DID YOU KNOW?

Another name for corn—a staple food in South America and Africa—is maize. Both corn and maize refer to the grass classified as *Zea mays*.

NUTRIENTS PER ⅔ CUP/3½ OZ FRESH RAW CORN KERNELS

Calories	88
Protein	3 g
Fat	0.8 g
Carbohydrate	20.7 g
Fiber	2.1 g
Vitamin B5	0.4 g
Choline	24 mg
Folate	36 mg
Niacin	1.7 mg
Vitamin C	6.4 mg
Magnesium	18 mg
Potassium	213 mg

Vegetable tart with a cornmeal crust

SERVES 4 ⓒ Ⓝ

olive oil, for greasing and
   brushing
3½ cups boiling water
1½ cups quick-cook polenta or
   cornmeal
1 tablespoon chopped fresh
   oregano, plus extra to garnish
1 small yellow bell pepper,
   seeded and thinly sliced
1 small red onion, thinly sliced
1 small zucchini, thinly sliced
2 tomatoes, sliced
4 ounces mozzarella cheese,
   diced
8 black ripe olives, pitted
   and halved
salt and pepper, to taste

Method

1 Preheat the oven to 400°F. Grease a large baking sheet. Pour the water into a large saucepan, add a pinch of salt, and bring to a boil over high heat. Add the polenta in a steady stream, stirring continuously until smooth. Reduce the heat and stir constantly for 4–5 minutes, or until the polenta is thick and smooth. Alternatively, prepare the cornmeal according to the package directions.

2 Remove from the heat and stir in the oregano. Season to taste with pepper. Spoon the cornmeal onto the prepared baking sheet and spread out in a 12-inch circle, raising the edges slightly.

3 Arrange the bell pepper, onion, zucchini, and tomatoes over the crust and add the mozzarella. Top the tart with the olives and brush lightly with olive oil.

4 Bake in the preheated oven for 15–20 minutes, or until bubbling and golden brown. Garnish with oregano and serve immediately.

04 MILLET

Tiny millet grains are versatile and pack a nutritional punch. They contain several nutrients that can be in short supply on a gluten-free diet.

Millet is particularly high in phosphorous—one of the nutrients highlighted as being in potential short supply on a gluten-free diet. It plays an important role in bone and nervous system maintenance, energy conversion from food, and in fat metabolism. A ⅓-cup/2¼-ounce portion of millet will give you around one-fifth of your daily needs. Millet is also a very good source of magnesium and B vitamins, which can be low in a gluten-free diet. Magnesium is essential for heart health, while vitamin B₅ helps your metabolism and folate helps proper brain function.

- Contains a good range of nutrients known to be low in the average gluten-free diet.
- Rich in phosphorous for bone health and fat metabolism.
- A good source of fiber and iron.
- Contains potassium for blood pressure control and muscle function.

Practical tips:
Cook millet as you would rice—in boiling water—until tender. Use it hot as an accompaniment to meats, poultry, and fish or use it cold in salads. Creamed millet, simmered in a mixture of milk and water until tender and creamy, is good with any dish in which you'd use cornmeal (see Corn, page 16). Add shredded cheese/chopped herbs for extra flavor. Add millet flour to your baked goods, including bread and muffins, or make into a flatbread.

DID YOU KNOW?

Millet was first eaten many thousands of years ago in North Africa, where it is still a staple grain today.

NUTRIENTS PER AVERAGE PORTION (⅓ cup/2¼ oz DRY WEIGHT) MILLET

Calories	227
Protein	6.6 g
Fat	2.5 g
Carbohydrate	43.7 g
Fiber	5.1 g
Vitamin B₅	2.8 g
Folate	51 mcg
Iron	1.8 mg
Magnesium	68 mg
Phosphorous	171 mg
Potassium	213 mg

Salmon packages with millet and spinach

SERVES 4 (V) (P) (N)

¾ cup millet, rinsed

4 salmon fillets, each about
   6 ounces and 1¼ inches thick

6-inch piece of leek, cut into
   matchsticks

1 carrot, cut into matchsticks

1 celery stalk, cut into
   matchsticks

1 tablespoon snipped
   fresh chives

6 tablespoons butter

7 cups baby spinach

salt and pepper, to taste

Method

1 Preheat the oven to 425°F and place a baking pan inside. Cut out four 13-inch squares of parchment paper.

2 Bring a saucepan of water to a boil. Add the millet and ½ teaspoon of salt. Bring back to a boil, then reduce the heat and simmer briskly for 10 minutes. Drain and set aside.

3 Place a salmon fillet in the center of each parchment paper square. Arrange the leek, carrot, and celery on top and sprinkle with the chives. Season with salt and pepper and dot with half the butter. Roll up the edges of the paper securely, allowing room in the package for steam to circulate.

4 Place the packages in the preheated baking pan and bake in the preheated oven for 12 minutes.

5 Meanwhile, heat the remaining butter in a skillet over medium–high heat. Stir in the cooked millet and the spinach and heat until the spinach has just wilted. Season with salt and pepper.

6 Divide the millet and spinach among four plates and transfer the contents of one of the packages on top of each. Serve immediately.

05

QUINOA

This little pseudo grain from South America is a perfect food to include on a gluten-free diet, because it has a superb nutritional profile and a great flavor.

Quinoa is one of the few "complete protein" plant foods, meaning it contains all nine essential amino acids. It's a particularly good plant source of lysine, which helps us absorb calcium and make hormones. Calcium is especially concentrated in quinoa—it contains more than twice the amount found in wheat. The seeds are rich in antioxidant compounds, including immune-boosting quercetin and anti-inflammatory kaempferol. Unlike other grain foods, quinoa is a good source of healthy fats. One-quarter is oleic acid (a heart-healthy fat) and it also contains alpha-linolenic acid (ALA), the omega-3 fat that can help reduce high cholesterol and blood pressure. Quinoa is also one of the easiest grains to digest, making it particularly useful for anyone with digestive problems.

- A complete source of protein.
- A useful source of calcium, antioxidants, and healthy fats.
- A good source of potassium, iron, magnesium, and zinc.
- A good source of the B-vitamin group, especially folate and B_1.

Practical tips:
Boil quinoa seeds in water until tender. For a nuttier flavor, dry roast or dry-fry for 5 minutes before boiling. Combine cooked, chilled quinoa with chopped vegetables, salads, beans, and herbs or spices for a healthy meal. Use instead of wheat in tabbouleh. You can buy quinoa noodles and flour as a healthy substitute for wheat grains in your baked goods. Quinoa is easy to sprout or puff (follow the directions given on packaging) or buy already prepared.

DID YOU KNOW?

Quinoa is not a cereal grain (a grass) at all, but the seed of a member of the beet family. Along with amaranth and buckwheat, it is sometimes termed a "pseudo cereal"—a product that looks like and can replace a true cereal in the diet.

NUTRIENTS PER AVERAGE PORTION (⅓ cup/2¼ oz DRY WEIGHT) QUINOA

Calories	221
Protein	8.5 g
Fat	3.6 g
Carbohydrate	38.5 g
Fiber	4.2 g
Vitamin B_1	0.2 g
Folate	110 mcg
Calcium	28 mg
Iron	2.7 mg
Magnesium	118 mg
Potassium	338 mg
Zinc	1.8 mg

Fruity puffed quinoa

SERVES 1   (C) (F) (V) (D) (N)

½ cup puffed quinoa
½ cup apple juice
1 small banana, thinly sliced
½ crisp, red-skinned apple,
   sliced into thin segments
2 teaspoons pumpkin seeds
honey, for drizzling
Greek yogurt, to serve (optional)

Method

1 Put the puffed quinoa into a serving bowl. Stir in the apple juice, making sure the puffs are submerged. Let stand for a few minutes.
2 Arrange the banana slices and apple segments on top of the quinoa.
3 Sprinkle with the pumpkin seeds and drizzle with a little honey. Serve immediately with yogurt, if using.

06

TEFF

One of the grains highest in protein, teff is also rich in minerals and contains a type of starchy fiber that is good for your digestive health.

Teff ranks with quinoa and amaranth in its high protein content, although it isn't regarded as a complete protein. It is high in bone-building calcium and in iron to help beat fatigue and for healthy blood. Perhaps most interesting is the fiber found in teff. Around 30 percent of teff's fiber is resistant starch, a relatively recently researched type of fiber that is helpful for diabetics, people with insulin resistance, and for anyone trying to lose weight, because it helps control insulin and blood sugar levels and keeps hunger at bay for longer. Teff is also the ideal grain for colon health—resistant starch produces a substance called butyrate in the colon, which is associated with a reduced risk of colon diseases, including cancer.

- One of the grains highest in protein.
- Rich in calcium and iron.
- High in resistant starch to help maintain blood sugar levels and a healthy colon.
- High levels of potassium to help regulate blood pressure.

Practical tips:
Traditionally, teff is ground into flour and used to make a spongy flatbread called *injera*. Try it as a single flour or mix with other gluten-free flours for pancakes, cookies, and wraps. Ivory-color teff has the mildest flavor; darker varieties have a stronger taste. Simmer the grains in water, as you would rice, and add to soups and stews.

DID YOU KNOW?

Tiny teff seeds have long been grown in Ethiopia and can grow in cold and wet areas where other grains don't thrive. The famed long-distance runners of Ethiopia eat teff for its ability to provide long-term energy.

NUTRIENTS PER AVERAGE PORTION (⅓ CUP/2¼ OZ DRY WEIGHT) TEFF

Calories	220
Protein	8 g
Fat	1.4 g
Carbohydrate	44 g
Fiber	4.8 g
Vitamin B$_5$	0.6 mg
Vitamin B$_6$	0.3 mg
Niacin	2 mg
Calcium	108 mg
Iron	4.6 mg
Magnesium	110 mg
Potassium	256 mg
Zinc	2.2 mg

Chocolate and ginger cookies

MAKES 12 (C) (N)

⅔ cup whole-grain teff flour
2 tablespoons gluten-free
   all-purpose flour
2 teaspoons unsweetened
   gluten-free cocoa powder
1 teaspoon ground ginger
½ teaspoon gluten-free
   baking powder
⅓ cup firmly packed light
   brown sugar
4 tablespoons butter, at
   room temperature
1 extra-large egg, beaten
1 ounce gluten-free semisweet
   chocolate, chopped
2 pieces of preserved ginger in
   syrup, drained and chopped
2 teaspoons ginger syrup

Method

1 Preheat the oven to 350°F and line a baking sheet with parchment paper. Put the flours, cocoa powder, ginger, and baking powder into a mixing bowl and combine thoroughly with a fork.

2 In another bowl, beat together the sugar and butter with a wooden spoon until pale and creamy—if the butter is soft it is quick and easy to do this. Add the egg, little by little, and beat until combined. Add a spoonful of the flour mixture if it looks like it is curdling.

3 Add the remaining flour mixture and combine with the wooden spoon. Stir in the chocolate, ginger pieces, and ginger syrup. Use a tablespoon to drop 12 spoonfuls of the dough onto the prepared baking sheet, leaving plenty of space between each because the cookies will spread. Place the sheet in the preheated oven and bake for 12 minutes.

4 Remove from the oven and use a spatula to transfer to a wire rack to cool completely.

07

SORGHUM

Sorghum, a grain that has been cultivated for thousands of years, is a rich source of several health-promoting plant chemicals.

It is only in recent years that the health benefits of sorghum have been researched, and it seems this grain has big potential to protect us from many diseases. It is rich in phytochemicals, including tannins, phenolic acids, anthocyanins, phytosterols, and policosanols. Policosanols are thought to be as effective as statins in lowering cholesterol, while a compound in sorghum called 3-DXA appears to stop the spread of colon cancer cells. Sorghum also contains antioxidant phenols linked with a reduction in the complications both of insulin resistance and diabetes, while the grain's tannins are said to reduce calorie absorption. And because sorghum is a low-GI food it may be useful for anyone watching their weight.

- Rich in plant chemicals linked with a variety of health benefits.
- High in a compound effective at reducing cholesterol.
- May be helpful to those watching their weight.

Practical tips:

Use sorghum in various dishes instead of rice, and cook it in a similar way. Try it in a tabbouleh with fresh herbs. You can also pop sorghum grains as you would corn for a healthy snack—try them sprinkled with paprika. Sorghum flour (the whole-grain version contains most nutrients) has a mild flavor and is excellent added to any gluten-free, mixed-grain flour for baking, because it can help improve the texture.

DID YOU KNOW?

Sorghum is the fifth most important cereal in the world, first harvested about 8,000 years ago in Egypt and arriving in the United States in the nineteenth century.

NUTRIENTS PER AVERAGE PORTION (⅓ cup/2¼ oz RAW WEIGHT) SORGHUM

Calories	203
Protein	6.8 g
Fat	2 g
Carbohydrate	44.8 g
Fiber	3.8 g
Niacin	1.8 mg
Calcium	17 mg
Iron	2.6 mg
Magnesium	166 mg
Potassium	210 mg
Zinc	2 mg

Seven-grain bread

MAKES 1 LOAF (C) (F) (V) (D) (N)

butter, for greasing
½ cup amaranth flour
¾ cup brown rice flour
⅔ cup sorghum flour
½ cup cornstarch
½ cup tapioca (cassava) flour
4 teaspoons ground chia seeds
1 cup ground flaxseed
2 teaspoons xanthan gum
2 teaspoons active dry yeast
1 teaspoon salt
3 eggs
1 tablespoon vegetable oil
2 tablespoons sugar
1 cup lukewarm water
1 tablespoon sunflower seeds

Method

1 Grease an 8½ x 4½ x 2½-inch loaf pan.
2 Combine together the flours, chia seeds, flaxseed, xanthan gum, yeast, and salt in a bowl.
3 In a separate bowl, mix together the eggs, oil, sugar, and water until well combined. Add the dry ingredients to the egg mixture and mix to form a soft dough.
4 Put the dough into the prepared pan, sprinkle with the sunflower seeds, and cover with a clean, damp dish towel for 1 hour or until the dough rises. Preheat the oven to 350°F.
5 Bake the loaf in the preheated oven for 40–45 minutes, until golden brown. Let cool in the pan for 5 minutes, then turn out onto a wire rack to cool completely.

08

CHICKPEA FLOUR

High in protein and with a broad range of important nutrients for the gluten-free diet, chickpea flour should definitely have a place in your kitchen.

Chickpea flour has been a staple food in India and the Middle East for many years, prized for its high protein (double that of wheat), carbohydrate content, and its many minerals. Made from chickpeas, or garbanzo beans, it has a similar nutritional profile and is an ideal addition to a gluten-free diet. It is one of the plant foods highest both in folate and choline, two B vitamins that reduce levels of harmful homocysteine (an amino acid thought to promote cardiovascular disease by damaging blood vessels and making blood more probable to clot) in the blood. It is also rich in magnesium, which can be low in a gluten-free diet. Deficiency can have a negative effect on the heart, blood pressure, bones, insulin function, sleep patterns, and general health so this flour is extremely beneficial.

- A high-protein, nutritious alternative to many more commonly used flours.
- Rich in folate and choline.
- Great source of magnesium.
- Contains many nutrients that may be lacking on a gluten-free diet.

Practical tips:
Chickpea flour, with its slightly nutty flavor, is used in India to make pakoras, poppadums, and bhajis. It is a high-protein alternative to wheat in many other recipes, including pancake batters, breads, and sauces, and can be used as an egg substitute in many baking recipes (beat together 3 tablespoons of chickpea flour with 3 tablespoons of water to replace each egg).

DID YOU KNOW?

Chickpea flour, made from ground chickpeas, is also called garbanzo bean flour and besan (look for this name in Indian grocery stores).

NUTRIENTS PER 1 CUP/3½ OZ CHICKPEA FLOUR

Calories	387
Protein	22 g
Fat	6 g
Carbohydrate	57 g
Fiber	10 g
Choline	95 mg
Folate	437 mcg
Niacin	1 mg
Vitamin E	0.5 mg
Calcium	45 mg
Iron	4 mg
Magnesium	166 mg
Potassium	846 mg
Zinc	2 mg

Spiced chickpea flour rolls

MAKES 24　Ⓒ Ⓕ Ⓥ Ⓓ Ⓟ Ⓝ

vegetable oil or peanut oil,
　for greasing
2¾ cups chickpea flour, sifted
½ cup plain yogurt
2½ cups warm water
2 teaspoons salt
¼ teaspoon ground turmeric
2 teaspoons grated fresh ginger
2 garlic cloves, crushed
4 teaspoons green chili paste

Topping

⅓ cup vegetable oil or peanut oil
1 teaspoon sesame seeds
1 teaspoon black mustard seeds
¼ cup finely chopped
　fresh cilantro
2 tablespoons freshly
　grated coconut

Method

1　Lightly brush four large baking sheets with oil and set aside.

2　Put the chickpea flour, yogurt, and water into a heavy saucepan with the salt, turmeric, ginger, garlic, and green chili paste. Whisk until smooth, then put over medium heat and continue to whisk constantly, for 5–6 minutes, until the batter starts to thicken, then reduce the heat to low, cover, and cook for 4–5 minutes. Stir, replace the lid, and cook for 2–3 minutes, or until thickened and smooth.

3　Remove from the heat and ladle the batter onto the prepared baking sheets, using a spatula to spread the batter as thinly as possible. The batter will start to set as it cools. Let stand for 5 minutes, then slice it lengthwise into 2-inch-wide strips to make about 24 rolls.

4　Starting at one end of each strip, use the spatula to gently lift and roll (like a small jellyroll). Repeat until all the strips have been rolled. Transfer to a serving plate.

5　Meanwhile, make the topping. Heat the oil in a skillet and add the sesame seeds and mustard seeds. When they start to pop, remove from the heat and drizzle this spiced oil over the chickpea flour rolls. Sprinkle with the cilantro and coconut. Serve warm or at room temperature.

09

SAGO STARCH

The small balls, or pearls, of sago starch are noteworthy for their high carbohydrate, low fiber content, and they are easy to digest.

Traditionally, sago starch was considered an ideal food for infants and people who were ill, convalescing, or elderly, because it is a particularly easy-to-digest food—high in pure carbohydrate with virtually no fiber, protein, or fat content. The pearls are also a useful food for anyone experiencing digestive problems associated with food allergies and anyone who wants to put on weight. In traditional herbal medicine, sago starch was recommended as a treatment for heat/acidity in the digestive system—today interpreted as indigestion. The starch has a small amount of iron and a little calcium.

- High in easily digested carbohydrate.
- A food almost anyone can eat without worrying about an allergy or intolerant reaction.
- Small iron and calcium content.
- Useful for anyone who wants to gain weight.

Practical tips:
Sago starch, like tapioca pearls, can be boiled with water or milk and sugar to make a sweet, cold dessert or hot pudding. When they are cooked, the "grains" become translucent. In India, sago starch is often fried in oil with onion, spices, herbs, and coconut and served as an unsweetened grain. Use sago flour to lighten gluten-free, mixed baking flours for cookies, cakes, and pancakes.

DID YOU KNOW?

Sago, originating from New Guinea, is obtained from the stems of the sago palm tree and processed into balls. Sago and tapioca are not from the same plant, although they look and taste similar.

NUTRIENTS PER AVERAGE PORTION (⅓ cup/2¼ oz DRY WEIGHT) SAGO STARCH

Calories	212
Protein	Trace
Fat	0.5 g
Carbohydrate	56 g
Fiber	0.3 g
Calcium	6 mg
Iron	0.7 mg

Blueberry and lime sago dessert

SERVES 4 (c) (d)

1¼ cups coconut milk
1¼ cups water
½ cup sago starch
⅓ cup shredded coconut
3 tablespoons sugar
grated zest and juice of 1 lime
1 teaspoon vanilla extract
½ teaspoon ground cinnamon
¼ teaspoon grated nutmeg
20 blueberries
⅓ cup diced fresh mango

Method

1 Bring the coconut milk and water to a boil in a saucepan over medium heat. Pour in the sago, stirring with a fork to keep the pearls separate. Turn down the heat and simmer on low for 20 minutes, stirring frequently to prevent the sago from sticking to the pan.

2 Meanwhile, put the coconut in a nonstick skillet over high heat, stirring occasionally, for 1 minute, or until it turns golden. Immediately remove from the heat and set aside.

3 When the sago has simmered for 20 minutes, add the sugar, lime zest, and half the juice, the vanilla extract, and spices. Stir well and simmer for an additional 10 minutes, or until the sago starch is virtually transparent and tender. If the mixture becomes too thick to simmer before the sago is cooked through, add a little boiling water and mix in thoroughly. When the sago is ready, take the pan off the heat and stir in the remaining lime juice. Let cool for 10 minutes.

4 Spoon the sago mixture into four stemmed glasses or ramekins and smooth the top with the back of the spoon. Cover and chill for 30 minutes–1 hour. Decorate each dessert with one-quarter of the toasted coconut, blueberries, and diced mango.

10 TAPIOCA

Mild-tasting tapioca is rich in starch that is easy to digest, and it is an ideal source of carbohydrate for anyone with digestive problems.

Tapioca is an unusual food—although its pearly appearance looks somewhat like a real grain, it comes from the root of the cassava plant and is then manufactured into the small white balls. Cassava (or manioc) root is extremely high in starch and has been cooked as an important source of calories and energy for people in certain countries, such as South America, Africa, and India, for centuries. Being easy to digest, it is often recommended as an ideal food to eat to gain weight and for people with digestive problems. Tapioca is not rich in vitamins or minerals, but it does contain a useful amount of iron and calcium and may contain small amounts of potassium, phosphorous, and magnesium.

- High starch, low-fat food.
- Easy to digest and low in fiber.
- Suitable for weight gain diets, especially for the elderly and those convalescing.
- Contains useful amount of calcium and iron.

Practical tips:
Tapioca pudding (made with milk, eggs, sugar, and vanilla) is probably the most famous use of the pearls in countries with a Western diet. Tapioca flour can be mixed half and half with rice flour to make a pancake batter or used in a gluten-free flour mix with denser flours for flatbreads and muffins. The flour is a useful gluten-free thickener for sauces and casseroles.

DID YOU KNOW?

Bubble (boba) tea, invented in Taiwan, is now a popular drink throughout Asia and in the United States. The most basic version is simply a milky tea, often with added sugar or syrup, with large tapioca pearls in the bottom.

NUTRIENTS PER AVERAGE PORTION (⅓ CUP/2¼ OZ DRY WEIGHT) TAPIOCA

Calories	215
Protein	Trace
Fat	Trace
Carbohydrate	53.2 g
Fiber	0.5 g
Calcium	12 mg
Iron	1 mg

Tapioca and potato cakes

MAKES 15–20   (**C**) (**D**)

2 potatoes, peeled and coarsely
    chopped
1⅓ cups medium tapioca pearls
1 cup cold water
2 fresh red chiles, finely chopped
1 teaspoon cumin seeds
1 teaspoon salt
¼ cup finely chopped
    fresh cilantro
vegetable oil or peanut oil,
    for deep-frying

Method

1 Put the potatoes into a saucepan of boiling water and boil for
12–15 minutes, or until just tender. Drain thoroughly and transfer
to a mixing bowl.

2 Meanwhile, put the tapioca in a bowl and pour the water over it. Let
soak for 12–15 minutes, until the water has been absorbed and the
tapioca is swollen. Transfer to a strainer to drain away excess liquid.

3 Add the chiles, cumin seeds, salt, and cilantro to the potatoes and
mash until fairly smooth. Stir in the soaked tapioca and mix well.
With wet hands, roll the mixture into 15–20 walnut-size balls, then
flatten to make patties.

4 Heat enough oil for deep-frying in a large saucepan or deep fryer
to 350–375°F, or until a cube of bread browns in 30 seconds.
Working in batches, deep-fry the tapioca and potato cakes for
3–4 minutes, or until golden brown. Remove with a slotted spoon
and drain on paper towels. Serve warm.

11

BROWN RICE

Nutrient-rich brown rice is a useful grain for a gluten-free diet because its mild flavor and good texture make it suitable for a wide range of dishes.

Rice is one of the most important grains for anyone on a gluten-free diet, because its high starchy carbohydrate content is a vital source of energy. While white rice contains few nutrients, brown rice has several nutritional benefits. It's a good source of dietary fiber to help reduce cholesterol and combat heart disease and it has a lower GI than many other grains. Brown rice also contains some protein and is a good source of the essential amino acids lysine and tryptophan (vital for building important proteins in the body). And it contains vitamin E and a range of the B vitamins (both of which can be in short supply in those not eating fortified wheat bread) and several minerals, including selenium and magnesium.

- Moderately low GI helps control blood sugar fluctuations.
- Good B-vitamin content to convert food into energy and keep the nervous system healthy.
- Rich in the antioxidant mineral selenium, which helps protect against some cancers.
- High in magnesium for a healthy heart and bone density.

Practical tips:
Brown rice is a perfect accompaniment to main dishes or for risottos and puddings, while rice noodles are ideal for Asian dishes and soups. Use brown rice flour to make great desserts and cookies, and to thicken sauces in sweet and savory dishes. Add rice flakes to muesli or use to make porridge. Rice will store in cool, dark, dry conditions in an airtight container for several months.

DID YOU KNOW?

Rice has been a staple food for half of the world's population for 6,000 years, but arrived in the United States only 400 years ago.

NUTRIENTS PER AVERAGE PORTION (⅓ CUP/2¼ OZ DRY WEIGHT) BROWN RICE

Calories	222
Protein	5 g
Fat	1.8 g
Carbohydrate	46 g
Fiber	3.6 g
Vitamin B₁	0.2 mg
Vitamin B₅	0.9 mg
Vitamin B₆	0.3 mg
Niacin	3 mg
Vitamin E	0.7 mg
Calcium	20 mg
Iron	0.8 mg
Magnesium	86 mg
Selenium	19.6 mcg
Zinc	1.3 mg

Chicken and brown rice salad

SERVES 4   Ⓒ Ⓕ Ⓥ Ⓟ Ⓝ

1¼ cups instant brown rice
2 teaspoons tomato paste
1 pound boneless, skinless
   chicken breast fillets
⅔ cup diced dried apricots
⅓ cup raisins
2 ounces pickled lemons,
   drained and finely chopped
1 small red onion, finely chopped
1¼ cups shredded kale
3 tablespoons pine nuts, toasted

Dressing
2 teaspoons harissa
¼ cup olive oil
juice of 1 lemon
salt and pepper, to taste

Method

1 Put the rice in a saucepan of boiling water. Bring back to a boil, then simmer for 25–30 minutes, or according to package directions, until tender. Drain, then transfer to a salad bowl.

2 Meanwhile, to make the dressing, put the harissa, oil, and lemon juice in a clean screw-top jar, season with salt and pepper, screw on the lid, and shake well.

3 Spoon 2 tablespoons of the dressing into a bowl and mix in the tomato paste. Preheat the broiler to high and line the broiler pan with aluminum foil. Put the chicken on the foil in a single layer. Brush some of the tomato dressing over the meat, and broil for 15–18 minutes, or until golden and cooked through, turning the meat and brushing it with the remaining tomato dressing halfway through cooking. Cut through the middle of a chicken breast to check that the meat is no longer pink and any juices run clear and are piping hot. Cover and let cool.

4 Drizzle the remaining dressing over the rice in the salad bowl. Add the dried apricots, raisins, pickled lemons, and onion, then toss gently together and let cool.

5 Add the kale and pine nuts to the salad and stir well. When cool, thinly slice the chicken, arrange on top of the salad, and serve.

12 RED RICE

Red rice makes a delicious change from brown rice in your diet, and the grains contain a high level of important antioxidants called anthocyanins.

There are several varieties of red rice grown across the world with slightly differing nutritional benefits, but they all contain the antioxidant group anthocyanins, and these give the rice its red coloring. These pigments have important health benefits—they are anti-inflammatory and can help reduce arthritis symptoms and they have anticarcinogenic activity so can protect against cancers. They can also help prevent cardiovascular disease, promote good vision, and help maintain a healthy weight and body-fat percentage. Red rice has a similar vitamin and mineral profile to brown rice, but it does vary, depending on the specific type you use—the nutrient values given here are only approximate.

• One of the only grains high in important anthocyanins.
• Excellent for people with arthritis, because eating it regularly can help reduce inflammation.
• Important for good vision.
• May help with weight loss and body-fat reduction.

Practical tips:
Most varieties of red rice can be cooked in exactly the same way as brown rice, although some may take less time—check the package directions. Red rice makes a real visual impact on the plate and is a good accompaniment to paler foods, such as white fish or chicken. It has a mild flavor and goes well with fruit and nuts in a salad. Camargue red rice is different from other varieties—it has a short grain and a nutty flavor and is excellent in risottos.

DID YOU KNOW?

One of the most highly prized types of red rice—Bhutan red rice—is grown 8,000 feet high up in the Himalayas. Irrigated with glacier water, it is said to contain more minerals than other varieties.

NUTRIENTS PER AVERAGE PORTION (⅓ CUP/2¼ OZ DRY WEIGHT) RED RICE

Calories	220
Protein	4.8 g
Fat	1.8 g
Carbohydrate	45 g
Fiber	2.4 g
Calcium	20 mg
Iron	0.5 mg
Magnesium	60 mg
Phosphorous	140 mg
Potassium	108 mg
Zinc	0.9 mg

Broiled shrimp with crisp-fried red rice

SERVES 4 Ⓥ Ⓟ Ⓝ

1 pound raw jumbo shrimp,
* peeled and deveined*
juice of 4 limes
1 small fresh red chile, seeded
* and finely chopped*
⅓ cup olive oil
⅔ cup Camargue red rice, rinsed
1¼ cups water
3 heads of red endive,
* leaves separated*
10–12 radishes, sliced
3 scallions, sliced
¼ cup red quinoa sprouts
salt and pepper, to taste

Method

1 Put the shrimp into a shallow dish. Stir in the lime juice, chile, and 2 tablespoons of the oil. Let marinate in the refrigerator for 2 hours.

2 Put the rice into a saucepan with the water and ½ teaspoon of salt. Bring to a boil, then cover and simmer for about 40 minutes, or according to the package directions. Fluff up with a fork and spread on a tray to dry.

3 Meanwhile, soak four wooden skewers in a shallow dish of water for at least 30 minutes. Preheat the broiler.

4 Transfer the rice to a skillet large enough to spread it out in a thin layer. Put it over medium-high heat and drizzle with the remaining oil. Cook for a few minutes, until a crust forms. Turn and cook for an additional few minutes. Keep warm over low heat until ready to serve.

5 Meanwhile, drain the shrimp, thread them onto the soaked skewers, and season with salt and pepper. Place them under the preheated broiler and cook for 5–6 minutes, until pink all over.

6 Divide the endive between four plates and top with the rice, radishes, and scallions.

7 Remove the shrimp from the skewers and arrange on top of the salad. Sprinkle with the quinoa sprouts and serve immediately.

13 WILD RICE

Wild rice—a slim, black grain that has become more widely available in recent years—is a unique food with several health benefits, especially for the heart, and a great addition to a gluten-free diet.

It contains nearly twice as much protein as brown rice and more than many other grains, so wild rice has a more beneficial effect on regulating blood sugar levels. It also contains a little more fiber and more iron—vital for transporting oxygen through our bodies and helping to prevent fatigue. The magnesium content—important for bone and heart health—is excellent. Wild rice also has 30 times more powerful antioxidant activity than white rice and can help lower total cholesterol and improve your blood lipids profile. It is a particularly good source of niacin, a B vitamin involved in the release of energy from food.

- A high-nutrient grain with many potential health benefits.
- Its high protein content makes it a useful grain for blood sugar stability and hunger prevention.
- High magnesium content for bone health.
- Several nutrients to help boost energy levels.

Practical tips:
Wild rice takes a long time to cook—up to an hour, depending on its age. With its nutty, smoky flavor, it is an ideal grain to mix with other rices or with quinoa or buckwheat, and it makes a great addition to salads. Leftover wild rice freezes well in a container or robust plastic freezer bag.

DID YOU KNOW?

Wild rice is not a true rice but seed from a grass that grows in marshy areas, especially in the United States.

NUTRIENTS PER AVERAGE PORTION (⅓ CUP/2¼ OZ DRY WEIGHT) WILD RICE

Calories	214
Protein	8.8 g
Fat	0.6 g
Carbohydrate	44.5 g
Fiber	3.7 g
Vitamin B$_5$	0.6 mg
Vitamin B$_6$	0.2 mg
Folate	57 mcg
Niacin	4 mg
Vitamin E	0.5 mg
Iron	1.2 mg
Magnesium	106 mg
Potassium	256 mg
Zinc	3.6 mg

Bean and wild rice salad

SERVES 6 　Ⓒ Ⓕ Ⓥ Ⓓ Ⓝ

1 cup wild rice
1 cup drained and rinsed,
  canned kidney beans
1 cup drained and rinsed,
  canned great Northern beans
1 cup drained and rinsed,
  canned navy beans
1 red onion, thinly sliced
4 scallions, finely chopped
1 garlic clove, crushed

Dressing
¼ cup olive oil
2 tablespoons balsamic vinegar
1 teaspoon dried oregano

Method

1 Place the rice in a large saucepan, cover with water, and bring to a boil. Reduce the heat then simmer for 45 minutes, or according to the package directions, until the rice is just tender and beginning to "pop." If necessary, add more boiling water as it cooks. When the rice is cooked, drain, refresh with cold water, and drain again.

2 To make the dressing, combine all the ingredients in a small bowl with a fork or small whisk.

3 Place all the beans in a large salad bowl with the onion, scallions, and garlic. Add the cooled rice and pour in the dressing. Mix together thoroughly, using a wooden or metal spoon. Chill in the refrigerator before serving.

Legumes

Legumes are a double blessing for anyone on a gluten-free diet, because they are rich both in carbohydrate and protein. One of them—the soybean—is a complete protein with a perfect balance of all the essential amino acids. Legumes are rich in various types of fiber to help the digestive system and all are rich in the B vitamins, antioxidant minerals, and plant chemicals to support good health.

(C) High in carbohydrate

(F) Good source of fiber

(V) Rich in vitamins and minerals

(D) Particularly good for digestive health

(P) High in protein

(N) Nutrient boost for gluten-free diet

14 ADZUKI BEANS

Adzuki beans are high in carbohydrates and rich in dietary fiber, protein, folate, and minerals, making them an ideal legume in a gluten-free diet.

Adzukis are a tasty way for gluten-free eaters to get a perfect balance of complex carbohydrates and protein. In addition, regular consumption of these small red beans offers cardiovascular benefits in a variety of ways. They are rich in soluble fiber, which helps lower blood cholesterol levels, and they also contain excellent amounts of magnesium, potassium, and folate, all of which support heart and arterial health. Adzuki beans are also rich in vitamin B_1, essential for metabolizing carbs into energy and to support nerve, muscle, and heart function.

- Perfect balance of carbohydrates and protein.
- Several heart-friendly nutrients and soluble fiber.
- Good source of vitamin B_1.
- Helps boost your calcium and zinc intake.

Practical tips:
Soak dried beans for 1 hour, then bring to a boil in fresh water for 10 minutes and simmer for 45 minutes, or until tender. Drain and cool to use in a bean salad. Alternatively, soak overnight, then sprout over several days, rinsing each day. These small beans are versatile and the dried beans can even be ground into a high protein flour with a sweet, nutty flavor that is ideal for baking cakes and cookies. In Asia, adzuki beans are often cooked to a soft consistency with coconut milk and used to add color, flavor, and protein to rice dishes.

DID YOU KNOW?

Adzukis are sometimes called red cowpeas. They are a staple in Japan and China, and in traditional Chinese medicine adzukis are said to bring strength and to offer support for the kidneys and reproductive organs.

NUTRIENTS PER AVERAGE PORTION (⅓ CUP/2¼ OZ DRY WEIGHT) ADZUKI BEANS

Calories	197
Protein	12 g
Fat	0.3 g
Carbohydrate	38 g
Fiber	7.6 g
Vitamin B_1	0.3 mg
Vitamin B_5	0.9 mg
Folate	373 mcg
Calcium	40 mg
Iron	3 mg
Magnesium	76 mg
Potassium	752 mg
Zinc	3 mg

Salsa bean dip

SERVES 4 (C)(F)(N)

12 cherry tomatoes, quartered
1 small red onion, finely chopped
1 cup drained and rinsed,
*   canned adzuki beans*
½ red bell pepper, seeded
*   and finely chopped*
½ or 1 red chile (to taste),
*   seeded and finely chopped*
2 teaspoons tomato paste
1 teaspoon agave nectar
large handful of chopped
*   fresh cilantro*
salt and pepper, to taste
4 small soft gluten-free tortillas,
*   to serve*
chili oil, to serve

Method

1 Put the tomatoes, onion, beans, red bell pepper, chile, tomato paste, agave nectar, and cilantro into a large bowl. Mix together well and season with salt and pepper.

2 Cover the bowl and let chill in the refrigerator for at least 15 minutes to let the flavors develop. Preheat the broiler to medium.

3 Place the tortillas under the preheated broiler and lightly toast. Let cool slightly, then cut into slices.

4 Transfer the bean dip to a small serving bowl. Serve with the sliced tortillas and chili oil to dip.

15

CANNELLINI BEANS

Firm-textured cannellinis are extremely rich in soluble fiber, which can help calm a sensitive digestive tract—a common problem for anyone with celiac disease.

An average ⅓-cup/2¼-ounce serving of cannellini beans will give you more than half of your RDA for total fiber, including a rich amount of soluble fiber, which can help calm a sensitive digestive system because it forms a gel in the digestive tract. This gel binds with cholesterol and helps remove it from our bodies, so cannellinis are also an excellent food for anyone with high cholesterol levels. The folate content helps to bring down levels of homocysteine in the blood, high amounts of which are harmful to the arteries, while magnesium and potassium help lower blood pressure. Good levels of iron help boost energy levels and lower the risk of anemia.

- Extremely rich in fiber and soluble fiber for a healthy digestive system and protection for the heart and arteries.
- High folate content helps remove harmful homocysteine from the blood.
- Can help reduce high blood pressure.
- Good source of iron.

Practical tips:

Soak dried beans overnight, then boil for 10 minutes in fresh water and simmer for 1½–2 hours, or until tender. Try them in soup or in a three-bean salad, or add them to a lamb casserole. They marry well with lemon juice, tomatoes, and garlic and are used in many classic Italian dishes.

DID YOU KNOW?

Cannellini beans (which are closely related to kidney beans) are one of Italy's favorite legumes, particularly in Tuscany—the Tuscan white bean and vegetable soup is famous around the world.

NUTRIENTS PER AVERAGE PORTION (⅓ CUP/2¼ OZ DRY WEIGHT) CANNELLINI BEANS

Calories	200
Protein	14.2 g
Fat	0.4 g
Carbohydrate	36 g
Fiber	14.9 g
Vitamin B₁	0.3 mg
Folate	236 mcg
Calcium	86 mg
Iron	4.9 mg
Magnesium	84 mg
Potassium	844 mg
Zinc	1.7 g

White chicken chili

SERVES 6　(**F**)(**D**)(**N**)

1 tablespoon vegetable oil

1 onion, diced

2 garlic cloves, finely chopped

1 green bell pepper, seeded
　　and diced

1 small green jalapeño pepper,
　　seeded and diced

2 teaspoons chili powder

2 teaspoons dried oregano

1 teaspoon ground cumin

1 teaspoon salt

2 (15-ounce) cans cannellini
　　beans, drained and rinsed

3 cups gluten-free chicken stock

3 cups shredded, cooked
　　skinless, boneless
　　chicken breasts

juice of 1 lime

⅔ cup chopped fresh cilantro

Method

1　Heat the oil in a large, heavy saucepan over medium-high heat. Add the onion, garlic, green bell pepper, and jalapeño and cook, stirring occasionally, for about 5 minutes, or until soft. Add the chili powder, oregano, cumin, and salt and cook, stirring, for about 30 seconds. Add the beans and stock and bring to a boil. Reduce the heat to medium-low and simmer gently, uncovered, for about 20 minutes.

2　Ladle about half of the bean mixture into a blender or food processor and puree. Return the puree to the pan along with the shredded chicken. Simmer for about 10 minutes, or until heated through. Just before serving, stir in the lime juice and cilantro. Serve immediately.

16 BLACK BEANS

Black beans are an ideal low-cost addition to a gluten-free diet—they contain a good balance of protein and carbohydrates and are rich in minerals and the B vitamins.

Black beans' extremely high fiber content—both soluble and insoluble—means they have strong cholesterol-lowering ability. They also contain several nutrients that play a part in maintaining the cardiovascular system. Their potassium content (which can help lower high blood pressure) is extraordinarily high, while they're also rich in magnesium (linked with protection from heart disease), folate, and choline (both of which reduce damaging homocysteine in the blood), and antioxidant anthocyanins (which reduce the risk of blood clots). These antioxidants may also reduce the risk of cancer and diabetes, while their prebiotic content maintains colon health.

- High fiber food to maintain colon health and reduce cholesterol.
- Several nutrients for cardiovascular health in excellent amounts.
- Rich in folate for healthy blood and development.
- An ideal balance of protein and carbohydrates.

Practical tips:
Dried black beans should be soaked for 8 hours, drained, added to fresh water, boiled for 5 minutes, and then simmered for around 1½ hours, or until tender. They have a slight mushroom flavor and are a tasty addition to a gluten-free diet. Try them fried and lightly crushed as a topping for baked potatoes or use them to give a Cuban twist to the classic Jamaican dish of rice and peas.

DID YOU KNOW?

A recent study found that adults who regularly eat beans weigh approximately 7 pounds less than nonlegume eaters, even though they consume 200 calories a day more.

NUTRIENTS PER AVERAGE PORTION (⅓ CUP/2¼ OZ DRY WEIGHT) BLACK BEANS

Calories	205
Protein	13 g
Fat	0.8 g
Carbohydrate	37.4 g
Fiber	9.1 g
Vitamin B₁	0.5 mg
Choline	40 mg
Folate	266 mcg
Calcium	74 mg
Iron	3 mg
Magnesium	103 mg
Potassium	890 mg
Zinc	2 g

Black bean and quinoa burritos

MAKES 8　(C)(F)(V)(D)

⅓ cup red quinoa, rinsed
⅔ cup water
2 tablespoons vegetable oil
1 red onion, diced
1 fresh green chile,
　seeded and diced
1 small red bell pepper,
　seeded and diced
1 (15-ounce) can black beans,
　drained and rinsed
juice of 1 lime
¼ cup chopped fresh cilantro
2 tomatoes
8 gluten-free corn tortillas,
　warmed
1 cup shredded cheddar cheese
1½ cups shredded romaine
　lettuce
salt and pepper, to taste

Method

1　Put the quinoa into a saucepan with the water. Bring to a boil, then cover and simmer over low heat for 15 minutes. Remove from the heat, but leave the pan covered for an additional 5 minutes to let the grains swell. Fluff up with a fork and set aside.

2　Heat the oil in a skillet. Sauté half the onion, half the chile, and all the red bell pepper until soft. Add the beans, cooked quinoa, and half the lime juice and cilantro. Sauté for a few minutes, then season with salt and pepper.

3　Halve the tomatoes and scoop out the seeds. Add the seeds to the bean mixture. Dice the tomato flesh and place in a bowl with the remaining cilantro, onion, chile, and lime juice, and season with salt. Stir.

4　Put about ⅓ cup of the bean mixture on top of each tortilla. Sprinkle each tortilla with an equal amount of the tomato salsa, cheese, and lettuce. Fold the end and sides over the filling, roll up, and serve immediately.

17

BLACK-EYED PEAS

Black-eyed peas rank among the top 40 foods rich in antioxidants, according to the U.S. Department of Agriculture, and they are rich in many minerals, too.

These pretty beans are high in flavonoids, a group of plant chemicals that help to keep our hearts and arteries healthy and can reduce the risk of cancer and boost the immune system. With an excellent carbohydrate content, they make a good alternative source of starch to gluten-free grains in the diet. The beans are some of the richest foods in potassium, a mineral that not only helps regulate blood pressure but is also important for healthy muscle function and bone strength, and in folate, for a healthy blood fats profile. Other nutrients found in black-eyed peas in good amounts are iron, zinc, and calcium.

- High in a range of flavonoids for heart and artery health and to protect against disease.
- High in complex carbohydrates.
- High in potassium and folate.
- A useful source of minerals, including iron, zinc, and calcium.

Practical tips:
Soak dried black-eyed peas for 4 hours before rapidly boiling for 5 minutes, then simmer for up to 2 hours, or until tender. You can enhance the quality of the protein in the beans by serving them with whole-grain rice or quinoa. They are also a good addition to a bean burger and make a tasty salsa (mix with chopped red onion, red bell pepper, fresh red chile, cilantro, and lime juice).

DID YOU KNOW?

Although black-eyed peas are perhaps most well-known as a component of soul food in the South, they were probably first grown in West Africa and Asia; they arrived in the United States in the seventeenth century.

NUTRIENTS PER AVERAGE PORTION (⅓ CUP/2¼ OZ DRY WEIGHT) BLACK-EYED PEAS

Calories	186
Protein	14 g
Fat	1 g
Carbohydrate	32.4 g
Fiber	5 g
Folate	378 mcg
Calcium	49 mg
Iron	4.6 mg
Magnesium	84 mg
Potassium	702 mg
Zinc	1.9 g

Bean and vegetable chili

SERVES 4   (F) (V) (N)

¼ cup gluten-free
  vegetable stock
1 onion, coarsely chopped
1 green bell pepper, seeded
  and finely chopped
1 red bell pepper, seeded and
  finely chopped
1 teaspoon finely chopped garlic
1 teaspoon finely chopped
  fresh ginger
2 teaspoons ground cumin
½ teaspoon chili powder
2 tablespoons tomato paste
1 (14½-ounce) can diced
  tomatoes
1 (15-ounce) can kidney beans,
  drained and rinsed
2 cups drained and rinsed,
  cooked black-eyed peas
salt and pepper, to taste
gluten-free tortilla chips, to serve

Method

1 Heat the stock in a large saucepan, add the onion and bell
  peppers, and simmer for 5 minutes, or until softened.
2 Add the garlic, ginger, cumin, chili powder, tomato paste, and
  tomatoes and stir to combine. Season with salt and pepper and
  simmer for 10 minutes.
3 Stir in all the beans and simmer for an additional 5 minutes, or until
  heated through thoroughly. Serve immediately with tortilla chips.

18

CRANBERRY BEANS

Because cranberry beans are particularly plentiful in fiber and a low-GI food, they are excellent for regulating blood sugar levels and keeping hunger at bay.

Cranberry beans are higher in dietary fiber, both soluble and insoluble, than many other beans and are, in fact, one of the highest-fiber foods of all. Fiber can be lacking in a gluten-free diet, so it's a good idea to eat legumes, including cranberry beans, regularly. Just one ⅓-cup/2¼-ounce serving can give you around half an adult's RDA. This fiber content means that the beans are digested slowly, not provoking a sharp rise in blood sugars. They are, therefore, low on the Glycemic Index, packed with slow-releasing energy, and will keep you feeling fuller for longer than most other carbohydrate foods. They will also help improve your blood fats profile if eaten regularly, and they are high in phosphorous to help maintain strong bones and teeth.

- Rich in soluble and insoluble fiber.
- Good food for regulating blood sugar levels and insulin secretion.
- High level of folate, vital for a healthy pregnancy and fetus.
- Phosphorous content helps bones and teeth.

Practical tips:
Cranberry beans have a nutty flavor and are delicious added to a bean salad with cannellini beans, fresh green beans, and a lemony dressing to complement the flavor. Soak dried beans overnight, then boil rapidly in fresh water for 10 minutes, drain, and rinse again before placing into a saucepan of fresh water and simmering for 1½–2 hours, or until tender.

DID YOU KNOW?

Cranberry beans are named for their mottled coloring, but these beans are also known as borlotti beans and are an important part of the Italian diet.

NUTRIENTS PER AVERAGE PORTION (⅓ CUP/2¼ OZ DRY WEIGHT) CRANBERRY BEANS

Calories	201
Protein	14 g
Fat	0.5 g
Carbohydrate	36 g
Fiber	14 g
Folate	362 mcg
Calcium	76 mg
Iron	3 mg
Magnesium	94 mg
Phosphorous	223 mg
Potassium	799 mg
Selenium	8.5 mcg
Zinc	2.2 g

Cranberry bean salad with eggs

SERVES 4   (F) (N)

1¼ cups dried cranberry
    beans, soaked overnight
    or for at least 8 hours
2 large garlic cloves, crushed
juice of 2 lemons
⅓ cup extra virgin olive oil
1 small onion, finely chopped
2 tomatoes, seeded and
    finely chopped
⅔ cup finely chopped fresh
    flat-leaf parsley
1 teaspoon cumin seeds,
    crushed
salt and pepper, to taste

Garnish

4 eggs
1 lemon, cut into 4 wedges
pinch of sumac or crushed
    red pepper flakes

Method

1 Drain and rinse the beans, put them in a large saucepan, cover
   with fresh cold water, and bring to a boil. Boil rapidly for at least
   10 minutes, then remove from the heat, drain, and rinse again.
   Add fresh cold water, bring to a boil, then simmer for 1½–2 hours,
   or until tender, adding more boiling water, if needed. Drain and
   transfer to a shallow serving dish.

2 For the garnish, put the eggs in a saucepan and pour in enough
   cold water to cover them by ½ inch. Bring to a boil, then reduce to
   a simmer and cook for 8 minutes. Drain immediately, cool quickly
   under cold running water, then peel and cut into quarters.

3 Lightly crush some of the warm beans with the back of a spoon.
   Add the garlic, lemon juice, olive oil, and 1 teaspoon of salt while
   the beans are warm, and mix together. Add the onion, tomatoes,
   parsley, and cumin seeds, season with pepper, then toss gently
   together. Arrange the hard-boiled eggs and lemon wedges on top,
   sprinkle with the sumac, and serve.

19

NAVY BEANS

High-fiber navy beans are one of the best legumes for all-round good nutrient content, providing protection against several diseases and health problems.

Navy beans are a high fiber food, over half of which is insoluble fiber—the type that ensures regular bowel movement and is linked with protection from digestive disorders, including diverticulitis and irritable bowel syndrome (IBS), and offers protection against colon cancer. The beans are particularly high in most of the important minerals, including iron (a 1/3-cup/2 1/4-ounce serving gives about one-quarter of your RDA), and magnesium (one-third of your RDA in a portion). The same portion size provides one-third of your RDA for Vitamin B_1, which has been shown to help improve digestive problems, such as ulcers and poor appetite. Navy beans are also high in tryptophan, the amino acid that helps the brain produce serotonin, the mood-improving chemical.

- Rich in insoluble fiber to protect from digestive disorders.
- Excellent source of iron and magnesium.
- Good source of a range of other nutrients, including calcium, zinc, and B_1.
- High in tryptophan to boost brain production of serotonin.

Practical tips:
Soak the dry beans for 8 hours, change the water, fast boil for 5 minutes, and then simmer for 1 1/2–2 hours, or until tender. Navy beans are one of the mildest in flavor of all the legumes, so they are best used in soups, casseroles, and composite dishes where they can soak up other flavors. They go particularly well with tomatoes, chile, olive oil, and lemon juice and with strong-tasting vegetables, such as kale.

DID YOU KNOW?

Navy beans, sometimes called white pea beans, Boston beans, or haricot beans, are the traditional bean used in Boston baked beans and canned baked beans.

NUTRIENTS PER AVERAGE PORTION (1/3 CUP/2 1/4 OZ DRY WEIGHT) NAVY BEANS

Calories	202
Protein	13.4 g
Fat	0.9 g
Carbohydrate	36.4 g
Fiber	14.6 g
Vitamin B_1	0.5 mg
Folate	218 mcg
Calcium	88 mg
Iron	3.4 mg
Magnesium	105 mg
Potassium	711 mg
Zinc	2.1 g

Squash and navy bean soup

SERVES 4 (C) (F) (V) (D) (P) (N)

1 teaspoon olive oil

1 red onion, chopped

2 garlic cloves, crushed

4 cups, peeled, seeded, and
chopped butternut squash
or pumpkin

2 teaspoons smoked paprika

¼ teaspoon crushed red
pepper flakes

5–6 fresh sage leaves, finely
chopped

3½ cups gluten-free vegetable
stock

1 (15-ounce) can navy beans,
drained and rinsed

salt and pepper, to taste

handful fresh flat-leaf parsley,
finely chopped, to garnish

Method

1 Heat the oil in a saucepan and sauté the onion and garlic for
3–4 minutes. Add the squash and cook for another 4–5 minutes.

2 Add the paprika, red pepper flakes, and sage and cook for about
1 minute, stirring all the time.

3 Pour in the stock and season with salt and pepper. Cover and
simmer for 20–25 minutes, or until the squash is tender. Let the
soup cool slightly, then process, using a handheld immersion
blender, until smooth.

4 Stir in the navy beans and heat through for 2–3 minutes. Serve
garnished with the parsley.

20

KIDNEY BEANS

Red kidney beans make a large starch and nutrient contribution to a gluten-free diet and are also high in plant sterols, with strong cholesterol-lowering power.

These popular beans, while not usually classified as a complete protein, contain the nine essential amino acids and are rich in complex carbohydrate, so they can replace grains as a gluten-free starch for your plate. Kidney beans are higher than most other natural foods in plant sterols, which help lower blood cholesterol by up to 15 percent. Extremely high in fiber, much of it insoluble, kidney beans can also keep your bowels regular and help protect against colon cancer. The fiber also gives the beans a low GI rating and makes them an ideal food for weight-loss plans and diabetics. Like many legumes, kidney beans are rich in several minerals, including one-quarter of your RDA for magnesium and zinc, and one-third of your RDA for iron in one ⅓-cup/2¼-ounce serving.

- Inexpensive source of good-quality protein.
- Rich in gluten-free starches and fiber.
- High in sterols to lower cholesterol.
- Good source of a range of important minerals.

Practical tips:
Soak dried kidney beans for 8 hours, then change the water and fast boil for at least 10 minutes to remove the toxin phytohaemagglutinin, which can cause severe illness. After boiling, simmer until cooked for 1–2 hours, or until tender. Kidney beans are a welcome addition to meat dishes, such as chili con carne, work well in veggie burgers, and make a good salad with other legumes, green beans, and an oil and vinegar dressing.

DID YOU KNOW?

Store dried kidney beans and other legumes in airtight containers in a cool, dry cupboard for up to a year or even longer. The older the bean, the longer it will take to cook.

NUTRIENTS PER AVERAGE PORTION (⅓ CUP/2¼ OZ DRY WEIGHT) KIDNEY BEANS

Calories	200
Protein	14 g
Fat	0.5 g
Carbohydrate	36 g
Fiber	14.9 g
Folate	236 mcg
Niacin	1.2 mg
Thiamin (B₁)	0.3 mg
Calcium	86 mg
Iron	4.9 mg
Magnesium	84 mg
Potassium	844 mg
Zinc	1.7 g

Three-bean energy-booster salad

SERVES 4   Ⓒ Ⓕ Ⓥ Ⓓ Ⓝ

2 cups halved green beans

1⅓ cups frozen edamame (soybeans) or frozen fava beans

1 cup frozen corn kernels

1 (15-ounce) can kidney beans, drained and rinsed

2 tablespoons chia seeds

Dressing

3 tablespoons olive oil

1 tablespoon red wine vinegar

1 teaspoon gluten-free whole-grain mustard

1 teaspoon agave syrup

4 teaspoons finely chopped fresh tarragon

salt and pepper, to taste

Method

1 Put the green beans, edamame, and corn kernels into a saucepan of boiling water. Bring back to a boil, then simmer for 4 minutes, until the green beans are just tender. Drain into a colander, rinse with cold water, then drain again and transfer to a salad bowl.

2 Add the kidney beans and chia seeds to the bowl and toss gently to mix together.

3 To make the dressing, put the oil, vinegar and mustard in a clean screw-top jar, then add the agave syrup and tarragon and season with salt and pepper. Screw on the lid and shake well. Drizzle the dressing over the salad, toss gently together, and serve immediately.

21 PINTO BEANS

These attractive beans with dark red markings are crammed with vitamins and minerals, particularly magnesium, potassium, and folate.

DID YOU KNOW?

Pinto means "painted" in Spanish—it was Spanish explorers who took the beans back to Europe from the Americas back in the Middle Ages.

NUTRIENTS PER AVERAGE PORTION (⅓ CUP/2¼ OZ DRY WEIGHT) PINTO BEANS

Calories	208
Protein	12.8 g
Fat	0.7 g
Carbohydrate	37.5 g
Fiber	9.3 g
Vitamin B₁	0.4 mg
Vitamin B₅	0.5 g
Vitamin B₆	0.3 g
Choline	39.7 mg
Folate	315 mcg
Niacin	0.7 mg
Calcium	68 mg
Iron	3 mg
Magnesium	106 mg
Phosphorous	247 mg
Potassium	836 mg
Zinc	1.4 mg

Like all legumes, pintos are high in fiber with all the health benefits that brings, and they are a particularly good food to add to a gluten-free diet, because they are a valuable source of starch. However, it is their excellent range and amount of minerals that makes them such a healthy food. They contain more magnesium than most other legumes—this mineral is not only vital for helping to control blood pressure but also helps maintain healthy nerves, bones, and muscles and is an immune booster. It also helps the body utilize the energy in foods and regulates blood sugar levels. Pinto beans also contain good amounts of the B vitamins, including choline for a healthy liver and to remove harmful homocysteine from the blood.

- Valuable source of starchy, high fiber carbohydrate for those on a gluten-free diet.
- High in magnesium with its range of health benefits.
- Rich in several other minerals and the B vitamins.
- Contains choline for healthy liver and blood.

Practical tips:
Soak dried pinto beans for 8 hours, then change the water and fast boil for 10 minutes. Change the water then simmer for 1½ hours, or until tender. Pintos have a pleasant, creamy texture and look attractive. Use in place of red kidney beans in a chili con carne or in a three-bean salad. Seasoned, pureed beans make a good filling for baked potatoes or sandwiches.

Country-style pinto beans with ham

SERVES 4   (F)(V)(P)(N)

2 tablespoons olive oil
1 large onion, chopped
2 green bell peppers, seeded
   and chopped
4 garlic cloves, crushed
1 teaspoon ground cumin
2½ cups cooked pinto beans
3 tablespoons ketchup
2 tablespoons packed
   dark brown sugar
2 tablespoons cider vinegar
2 teaspoons gluten-free
   Worcestershire sauce
2 teaspoons gluten-free
   French-style mustard
⅔ cup gluten-free vegetable
   stock or chicken stock
2 cups cubed cooked ham
salt and pepper, to taste
2 tablespoons chopped fresh
   flat-leaf parsley, to serve
cooked brown rice, to serve

Method

1 Heat the oil in a flameproof casserole dish or Dutch oven set over medium-low heat, add the onion and bell peppers, and cook for 5 minutes, stirring occasionally. Add the garlic and cumin, stir to combine, and cook for an additional minute.

2 Stir in the beans, ketchup, sugar, vinegar, Worcestershire sauce, mustard, stock, and ham, combining everything well. Bring to a simmer, cover with a lid, and cook gently for 45 minutes.

3 Season with salt and pepper and sprinkle the parsley over the top. Serve with brown rice.

22 CHICKPEAS

Chickpeas, which are also called garbanzo beans, are a high-fiber source of complex carbs and protein, and they have a strongly beneficial effect on blood fats, the digestive system, and insulin.

DID YOU KNOW?

A popular way to eat chickpeas is as hummus, the nutrient-rich dip originating in Middle Eastern countries, such as Morocco, and made with tahini (sesame seed paste), garlic, and olive oil.

NUTRIENTS PER AVERAGE PORTION (⅓ CUP/2¼ OZ DRY WEIGHT) CHICKPEAS

Calories	218
Protein	11.6 g
Fat	3.6 g
Carbohydrate	36.4 g
Fiber	10.4 g
Vitamin A	12 mcg
Vitamin B₁	0.3 mg
Vitamin B₅	1 g
Vitamin B₆	0.3 g
Choline	57 mg
Folate	334 mcg
Niacin	0.9 mg
Vitamin E	0.5 mcg
Calcium	63 mg
Iron	3.7 mg
Magnesium	69 mg
Potassium	525 mg
Zinc	2 mg

Chickpeas appear to be good at improving the balance and type of fats in our blood. In recent trials, regular consumption gave the testers lower total and LDL cholesterol and reduced triglyceride levels, compared with people who ate other types of high-fiber food. Chickpeas also have a positive effect on insulin and blood sugar levels, so they are a recommended food for diabetics. Their high fiber content supports the digestive system and can help prevent diverticulitis and colon cancer, while the plant chemicals chickpeas contain—isoflavones, saponins, and phytosterols—protect against both heart disease and cancers. They also contain other heart-friendly nutrients, including magnesium and folate.

- High in fiber to support the digestive system.
- Good source of most of the B vitamins, including folate.
- Rich in minerals, including iron, zinc, magnesium, potassium, and calcium.
- Contains several plant chemicals to fight heart disease and cancer.

Practical tips:
Soak dried chickpeas for 4 hours or more before boiling for 5 minutes and then simmering for 1½ hours, or until soft. Canned cooked chickpeas have a similar nutrient profile to those cooked from raw. Try using them in a vegetable Moroccan stew with butternut squash, green bell peppers, apricots, and harissa.

Spicy falafels

SERVES 4 (F) (P) (N)

1 (15-ounce) can chickpeas,
*   drained and rinsed*
1 small red onion, chopped
2 garlic cloves, crushed
2 teaspoons ground coriander
1½ teaspoons ground cumin
1 teaspoon ground star anise
1 fresh red chile, chopped
1 egg white
½ teaspoon gluten-free
*   baking powder*
chickpea (besan) flour,
*   for shaping*
sunflower oil, for deep-frying
salt and pepper, to taste

Salad

1 large orange
2 tablespoons extra virgin
*   olive oil*
3 cups arugula leaves
salt and pepper, to taste

Method

1 Put the chickpeas, onion, garlic, coriander, cumin, anise, chile, egg white, and salt and pepper in a blender or food processor and process to a firm, but still textured, paste. Stir in the baking powder.

2 Use a little chickpea flour on your hands to shape the mixture into 12 small balls.

3 To make the salad, cut all the peel and white pith from the orange and lift out the segments, catching the juice. Whisk the orange juice with the olive oil and season with salt and pepper. Lightly toss the orange segments and arugula with the dressing.

4 Heat a 1-inch depth of oil in a large pan to 350°F, or until a cube of bread browns in 30 seconds. Cook the falafels for about 2 minutes, until golden brown.

5 Drain the falafels on paper towels and serve with the salad.

23 SPLIT PEAS

Split peas are a sweet-tasting, quick-cook legume and make an ideal nutrient-rich addition to a meal to supply carbs in a gluten-free diet.

DID YOU KNOW?

Both green and yellow split peas have a similar nutrient profile. They are both varieties of the same plant, *Pisum savitum*, which has been cultivated for around 12,000 years.

NUTRIENTS PER AVERAGE PORTION (⅓ CUP/2¼ OZ DRY WEIGHT) SPLIT PEAS

Calories	205
Protein	14.7 g
Fat	0.7 g
Carbohydrate	36 g
Fiber	15.3 g
Vitamin A	26 mcg
Vitamin B₁	0.4 mg
Vitamin B₅	1 mg
Vitamin B₆	0.3 g
Choline	57 mg
Folate	164 mcg
Niacin	1.7 mg
Calcium	33 mg
Iron	2.6 mg
Magnesium	69 mg
Phosphorous	220 mg
Potassium	589 mg
Zinc	1.8 mg
Beta-carotene	53 mcg

While the amount of some of the minerals is not as high as in some other legumes, split peas contain more vitamin A, which is important for good vision and skin, and some beta-carotene, which converts to vitamin A in our bodies. They are also particularly high in niacin and choline (two B vitamins that improve the blood fats profile), potassium (for healthier blood pressure levels), and phosphorous (for strong teeth). Rich in total and soluble fiber, split peas help ease digestive upsets and improve bowel function. They also contain isoflavones, which may help reduce the risk of some cancers, and phytosterols which can lower cholesterol.

• Rich in several nutrients and chemicals to improve blood and heart health.
• A useful source of vitamin A.
• Fiber helps ease bowel problems and digestive upsets.
• Plant chemicals help to lower cholesterol and reduce the risk of some cancers.

Practical tips:

Split peas are quick to cook and don't even need to be presoaked. Add them to boiling water and simmer for 25 minutes, or until tender, or add them straight into the pan as they are for quick-and-easy soups and casseroles. Split pea dal is a spicy Indian dish often served with rice, and makes a healthy, cost-effective meal.

Split pea and ham soup

SERVES 6–8   (C) (F) (V) (D) (P) (N)

2¾ cups split green peas
1 tablespoon olive oil
1 large onion, finely chopped
1 large carrot, peeled and
    finely chopped
1 celery stalk, finely chopped
4 cups gluten-free chicken or
    vegetable stock
4 cups water
2 cups finely diced,
    lean unsmoked ham
¼ teaspoon dried thyme
¼ teaspoon dried marjoram
1 bay leaf
salt and pepper, to taste

Method

1 Rinse the peas under cold running water. Put them into a saucepan and cover generously with water. Bring to a boil and boil for about 3 minutes, skimming off any foam that rises to the surface with a slotted spoon. Drain and set aside.

2 Heat the oil in a large saucepan. Add the onion and cook over medium heat for 3–4 minutes, until just softened.

3 Add the carrot and celery and cook for 2 minutes. Add the peas, pour in the stock and water, and stir to combine. Bring just to a boil and stir the ham into the soup.

4 Add the thyme, marjoram, and bay leaf to the pan. Reduce the heat, cover, and cook gently for 1–1½ hours, until everything is soft. Remove and discard the bay leaf. Taste and adjust the seasoning, if necessary. Ladle into warm soup bowls and serve.

24 RED LENTILS

High in plant sterols and soluble fiber, red lentils are one of the best legumes for anyone with digestive problems. The high iron and zinc content also makes this legume a valuable addition to a gluten-free diet.

A good source of beta-sitosterol, a plant compound that lowers LDL cholesterol in the blood and is not easy to find in many natural foods, red lentils are also a good source of easily-digested starch. They are lower in total fiber than green or brown lentils, but the proportion of cholesterol-lowering soluble fiber is a little higher. The reduced fiber content makes these lentils a good choice for anyone with a particularly sensitive digestive tract, prone to bloating and/ or loose bowels. Red lentils are rich in iron, which can be in short supply on a gluten-free diet. Iron is important for healthy blood and to prevent tiredness and anemia. Their zinc content is impressive – one ⅓-cup/2¼-ounce portion provides a quarter of a day's RDA of this important immune-booster.

- High in easily digested starch and soluble fiber.
- Source of beta-sitosterol which can lower LDL cholesterol.
- Rich in energy-promoting iron.
- High in the antioxidant zinc to boost the immune system.

Practical tips:
Pureed red lentils form the basis of the most popular version of the Indian spiced dish, dal. Eaten with rice, this makes a high-quality protein meal. Red lentils are usually cooked within 25 minutes and need no soaking, so they make a quick and pretty soup (try adding to carrot, potato, onion, and cilantro) or a hearty pâté.

DID YOU KNOW?

The older the lentils are, the longer they will take to cook down to a rich, yellow puree. Rinse dry lentils in cold water before cooking and pick over to remove any shrivelled lentils or stems.

NUTRIENTS PER AVERAGE PORTION (⅓ CUP/2¼ OZ DRY WEIGHT) RED LENTILS

Calories	207
Protein	14.9 g
Fat	1.3 g
Carbohydrate	35.4 g
Fiber	6.5 g
Vitamin B₁	0.3 mg
Vitamin B₆	0.2 mg
Folate	122 mcg
Niacin	0.9 mg
Calcium	25 mg
Iron	4.5 mg
Magnesium	43 mg
Phosphorous	176 mg
Potassium	347 mg
Selenium	4.9 mcg
Zinc	2.4 mg

Spicy carrot and lentil soup

SERVES 4   Ⓒ Ⓕ Ⓥ Ⓓ Ⓟ Ⓝ

2 tablespoons olive oil

1 large onion, chopped

1 celery stick, chopped

1 potato, diced

6 carrots, sliced

1 teaspoon paprika

2 teaspoons ground cumin

1 teaspoon ground coriander

½ teaspoon chili powder, plus
   extra to taste (optional)

1 cup red split lentils

5 cups gluten-free
   vegetable stock

2 bay leaves

salt and pepper, to taste

fresh cilantro leaves,
   to garnish

Method

1 Heat the oil in a large, heavy saucepan over medium-low heat. Add the onion and sauté for 7 minutes, stirring occasionally. Add the celery, potato, and carrots and cook for an additional 5 minutes, stirring occasionally. Stir in the paprika, cumin, ground coriander, and chili powder, if using, and cook for an additional minute.

2 Stir in the lentils, stock, and bay leaves. Bring to a boil, then reduce the heat and simmer, half-covered, over low heat, stirring occasionally to prevent the lentils from sticking to the bottom of the saucepan. Cook for 25 minutes, or until the lentils are tender.

3 Remove and discard the bay leaves. Transfer to a food processor or blender, or use a handheld immersion blender, and process the soup until smooth. Return to the saucepan and reheat. Season with salt and pepper and add extra chili powder, if desired. Ladle into warm bowls and garnish with cilantro before serving.

25

GREEN/BROWN LENTILS

Both high in protein and carbohydrate, green and brown fiber-rich lentils are a tasty way to boost your B-vitamin and mineral intake.

NUTRIENTS PER AVERAGE PORTION (⅓ CUP/2¼ OZ DRY WEIGHT) GREEN OR BROWN LENTILS

Calories	212
Protein	15.5 g
Fat	0.6 g
Carbohydrate	36 g
Fiber	18 g
Vitamin B$_1$	0.5 mg
Vitamin B$_6$	0.3 mg
Folate	287 mcg
Niacin	1.6 mg
Calcium	34 mg
Iron	4.5 mg
Magnesium	73 mg
Potassium	573 mg
Selenium	5 mcg
Zinc	2.9 mg

Black, brown, and deep green lentils tend to have a similar nutrient content and levels. Lentils are a rich source of both insoluble and soluble fiber and isoflavones (all of which help protect against cancer and cardiovascular disease), and lignans, plant compounds with mild estrogen-like effect, which may help keep bones strong as we age. They are rich in the B vitamins for nerve health and folate for the reproductive system, and they are higher in the antioxidant, anticancer mineral selenium than most of the dried legumes. And their high potassium content can help regulate the heartbeat and reduce high blood pressure.

- Rich in dietary fiber for protection from cardiovascular disease.
- Lignans help keep bones strong and selenium can protect against cancer.
- Great source of several of the B vitamins.
- High in potassium for healthy heart.

Practical tips:
Lentils are one of the few legumes that don't need soaking and are usually tender after only 30–40 minutes simmering. Cook them in the pot with meat and/or vegetables for an easy stew. They also make excellent burgers or a nutrient-rich soup.

Tuna, lentil, and potato salad

SERVES 4 Ⓒ Ⓕ Ⓥ Ⓓ Ⓟ Ⓝ

1 cup green or brown lentils

2 tablespoons olive oil, plus extra for brushing

12 ounces baby new potatoes, halved

1 small butterhead lettuce

4 fresh tuna steaks, about 4 ounces each

2 cups halved cherry tomatoes

2 cups arugula

Dressing

⅓ cup fruity olive oil

1 tablespoon balsamic vinegar

2 teaspoons red wine vinegar

1 teaspoon smooth, gluten-free Dijon mustard

1 teaspoon honey

Method

1 Boil the lentils in a saucepan of water for about 30 minutes, or until tender. Drain, transfer to a salad bowl, and stir in the olive oil.

2 Put the potatoes in a saucepan and cover with cold water. Bring to a boil, cover, and simmer for 15 minutes, or until tender. Drain well.

3 Meanwhile, break the outer lettuce leaves off the lettuce and cut the heart into eight pieces. Arrange on four plates.

4 To make the dressing, put all the ingredients in a clean screw-top jar, screw on the lid, and shake well.

5 Preheat a ridged grill pan over high heat. Brush the tuna with olive oil. Cook it in the hot pan for 3 minutes for rare or 5 minutes for medium, turning once. Transfer it to a plate and cut each steak into six chunks.

6 Arrange the lentils, tuna, potatoes, and tomatoes over the lettuce, sprinkle with the arugula and spoon the dressing over the salad. Serve immediately.

26 SOYBEANS

Rich in high-quality protein, soybeans
also contain good amounts of minerals,
the B vitamins, and a range of plant
chemicals to help keep you healthy.

Soybeans are unusual in that they contain all nine of the amino
acids—the "building blocks of protein"—in amounts comparable
to that in animal protein. Unlike most legumes, soybeans are
moderately high in fat, most of which is unsaturated and 8 percent
of which is the omega-3 fat, ALA, for heart health. They also
contain other nutrients (such as potassium, magnesium, zinc,
and choline) that protect the heart and several plant chemicals
(isoflavones, phytosterols, betaines, and saponins) that combat
heart disease or cancer. Tofu (or bean curd) is a high-protein,
low-calorie food processed from soybeans. It has fewer vitamins
and minerals than the natural beans but still contains a good
amount of calcium.

- Plant source of high-quality "complete" protein.
- Contains omega-3 fats.
- Rich in several nutrients and fiber for heart health.
- Good content of the anticancer mineral, selenium.

Practical tips:
Soybeans need long soaking—at least 8 hours—then boiling in
fresh water for 10 minutes and simmering for around 2 hours, or
until tender. Drain and use the beans in soups, stir-fries, and stews,
or add mashed beans to veggie burgers. Tofu can be bland on its
own but is delicious when marinated—broil, stir-fry, add to curries,
or eat as it is. High protein soy flour can be used in baking.

DID YOU KNOW?

Tofu was first made from
soybeans in China around
2,000 years ago. The process
has much in common with
that of making cheese.

NUTRIENTS PER AVERAGE PORTION (⅓ CUP/ 2¼ OZ DRY WEIGHT) SOYBEANS

Calories	268
Protein	22 g
Fat	12 g
Carbohydrate	18 g
Fiber	5.6 g
Vitamin B$_1$	0.5 mg
Vitamin B$_6$	0.5 mg
Choline	69.5 mg
Folate	225 mcg
Niacin	1 mg
Calcium	166 mg
Iron	9.4 mg
Magnesium	168 mg
Potassium	1,078 mg
Selenium	10.7 mcg
Zinc	2.9 mg

Miso and tofu salad

SERVES 4   (F) (V) (P)

1 pound firm tofu, drained
    and cut into ½-inch slices
1 tablespoon sesame seeds
1 cup thinly sliced snow peas
1 cup bean sprouts
12 asparagus spears, trimmed
    and cut into long, thin slices
1 zucchini, cut into matchsticks
1 small butterhead lettuce,
    leaves separated and cut
    into long slices
1 cup coarsely chopped
    fresh cilantro
3 cups mixed sprouts, such
    as alfalfa sprouts and
    radish sprouts

Dressing

3 tablespoons rice wine vinegar
2 tablespoons gluten-free
    soy sauce
3 tablespoons sunflower oil
1 tablespoon gluten-free sweet
    white miso
2 garlic cloves, finely chopped

Method

1 For the dressing, put the vinegar and soy sauce in a clean screw-top
jar and add the oil, miso, and garlic. Screw on the lid and shake.

2 Preheat the broiler to high and line the broiler pan with aluminum
foil. Put the tofu on the foil in a single layer. Mark crisscross lines
over each slice using a knife, then sprinkle with the sesame seeds.
Spoon over half the dressing, then broil for 8–10 minutes, turning
once, until browned.

3 Put the snow peas, bean sprouts, asparagus, zucchini, and lettuce
on a plate. Pour the remaining dressing over them and toss gently
together. Sprinkle with the cilantro and sprouts, then top with the
hot tofu, drizzle with any pan juices, and serve immediately.

Nuts and seeds

While nuts and seeds are almost all high in healthy fats, a rich source of calories, and a good source of protein, they each offer a different range of textures, flavors, and nutrients. From the special fats and antibiotics in coconuts through to the anti-inflammatory form of vitamin E found in pumpkin seeds and the high levels of omega-3s in walnuts, this food group is invaluable in your diet and can be enjoyed in many dishes.

(C) High in carbohydrate

(F) Good source of fiber

(V) Rich in vitamins and minerals

(D) Particularly good for digestive health

(P) High in protein

(N) Nutrient boost for gluten-free diet

27 COCONUT

The creamy white flesh of the coconut is high in fat, much of which is a type of saturated fat that is antibiotic and good for you.

More than 80 percent of the calories in coconut are from fat and, although much of this fat is saturated, there is emerging evidence that they are healthy fats of which there are few dietary sources. Several studies show they reduce the risk of cardiovascular disease. One of these fats, lauric acid, seems to have the ability to increase the "good cholesterol" HDL in the blood. Coconut fats also seem to have a strong antibiotic effect, and there is anecdotal evidence that coconut oil may even reverse or postpone the effects of Alzheimer's disease. The nut also contains phytosterols, which have a total cholesterol-lowering effect, and coconut flesh is a good source of fiber.

- One of the few sources of dietary medium-chain fats linked to heart protection.
- Can increase HDL cholesterol.
- Strongly antibiotic.
- May improve symptoms of Alzheimer's disease.

Practical tips:
Coconut flour and dried coconut are both dried forms of coconut good for keeping in the pantry. Use the flour in baking but follow coconut-specified recipes to be sure of good results. You can drink coconut water (the clear liquid inside a whole coconut) as it is, while coconut milk is made by pressing coconut flesh to produce a milky liquid and is used in many Asian dishes.

DID YOU KNOW?

Coconut oil is one of the best and healthiest fats you can use for frying. Solid at room temperature, it is slower to oxidize and alter chemically than other cooking oils, particularly those high in polyunsaturated fats. Oxidized fats are thought to contribute to heart disease.

NUTRIENTS PER
2 x 2-INCH PIECE/1¾ OZ
FRESH COCONUT

Calories	177
Protein	1.7 g
Fat	16.7 g
Carbohydrate	7.6 g
Fiber	4.5 g
Iron	1.2 mg
Potassium	178 mg
Selenium	5 mcg

NUTRIENTS PER
1 TABLESPOON
COCONUT OIL, COLD-PRESSED

Calories	117
Protein	13.6 g

Coconut and mango quinoa

SERVES 4   (**F**)

1¼ cups canned coconut milk
⅔ cup white quinoa, rinsed
1 large ripe mango
    (about 1¼ pounds)
⅓ cup sugar
juice of 1 large lime
1½-inch piece fresh ginger,
    sliced into chunks
⅔ cup blueberries
¼ cup toasted coconut chips
4 lime wedges, to decorate

Method

1 Put the coconut milk and quinoa into a small saucepan over medium heat and bring to a boil. Reduce the heat, cover, and simmer for 15–20 minutes, or until most of the liquid has evaporated. Remove from the heat, but leave the pan covered for an additional 10 minutes to allow the grains to swell. Fluff up with a fork, transfer to a bowl, and let cool.

2 Meanwhile, peel the mango, discard the pit, and coarsely chop the flesh (you will need 2 cups). Put the mango into a food processor with the sugar and lime juice. Squeeze the ginger in a garlic press and add the juice to the mango mixture. Process for 30 seconds to make a smooth puree.

3 Mix the mango mixture into the cooled quinoa and let stand for 30 minutes.

4 Divide the mixture among four bowls and sprinkle with the blueberries and coconut chips. Decorate with lime wedges and serve.

28 ALMONDS

Almonds, like many nuts, are a high fat food but this is mostly the heart-protective monounsaturated type. Almonds protect your heart in other ways, too.

The fat in almonds is more than 60 percent monounsaturated and strongly linked with protection from heart disease by its ability to improve the blood fats profile by lowering LDL and raising HDL. Almonds are also rich in vitamin E—one ⅓-cup/1¾-ounce portion contains more than your RDA—and in flavonoids, both of which offer additional protection for the cardiovascular system. Vitamin E's other benefits include protection from cancer, skin problems, and arthritic aches and pains. A good source of calcium, the same serving of almonds provides around one-fifth of your daily needs. And research shows that a handful of almonds a day can help people with type-2 diabetes to regulate their blood glucose levels.

- An excellent source of healthy monounsaturated fats.
- Rich in the antioxidant vitamin E.
- A great source of nondairy calcium.
- Rich in flavonoids, which offer protection for the heart.

Practical tips:
Try to find whole almonds with their brown skins still on—the skins contain most of the beneficial flavonoids and vitamin E, and also help the nuts to stay fresh. Almonds can be used in many sweet and savory dishes and make an ideal topping for breakfast cereals or a portable snack. The oil can be used in a salad dressing, while almond flour is a useful high-protein flour for the gluten-free diet—try it in cookies, crumb toppings, and cakes. Store nuts, oil, and flour in a cool place to retain the health-giving compounds.

DID YOU KNOW?

Overweight people on diets who regularly eat almonds lose weight more quickly than those who don't. Women who ate nuts at least five times a week had a 30 percent reduction in diabetes risk over women who never ate nuts, according to one American study.

NUTRIENTS PER ⅓ CUP/1¾ OZ FRESH SHELLED ALMONDS

Calories	288
Protein	10.6 g
Fat	24.7 g
Carbohydrate	10.8 g
Fiber	6.1 g
Vitamin B₂	0.15 mg
Folate	25 mcg
Niacin	1.7 mg
Vitamin E	13 mg
Calcium	132 mg
Iron	1.9 mg
Magnesium	134 mg
Potassium	353 mg
Zinc	1.5 mg

Clementine almond cake

SERVES 8–10   ⓒ

*1 stick unsalted butter,
   plus extra for greasing*
⅔ cup sugar
4 eggs, separated
1 cup millet flour
*2 teaspoons gluten-free
   baking powder*
*1¼ cups ground almonds
   (almond flour)*
*juice and finely grated zest
   of 2 clementines*

Syrup
juice of 4 clementines
½ cup sugar

Topping
1 cup low-fat cream cheese
2 tablespoons sugar
2 tablespoons heavy cream

Method

1 Preheat the oven to 350°F. Grease a 9-inch springform cake pan.

2 Beat together the butter and sugar for 3 minutes, until fluffy. Gradually beat in the egg yolks.

3 Combine the flour, baking powder, and ground almonds, then beat into the butter, sugar, and egg yolk mixture. Mix in the clementine juice, reserving the zest.

4 Whisk the egg whites until they hold stiff peaks. Fold carefully into the mixture, using a large metal spoon. Spoon the batter into the prepared pan.

5 Bake in the preheated oven for 30–40 minutes, until a toothpick inserted into the center comes out clean.

6 Meanwhile, to make the syrup, put the clementine juice and sugar into a small saucepan and bring to a boil. Boil for 3 minutes, until syrupy.

7 With the cake still in its pan, make holes all over the surface with a toothpick. Pour the hot syrup over the cake. When it has trickled into the holes, remove the cake from the pan and transfer to a wire rack to cool completely.

8 To make the topping, beat together the cream cheese, sugar, and cream. Spread the topping over the cake and sprinkle with the reserved clementine zest.

29

CHESTNUTS

Chestnuts are low in fat and calories, and their high carbohydrate content makes them ideal for use in a gluten-free diet, either as nuts or as a flour.

Compared with other nuts, they are unusually rich in starches, which means that their sweet flesh is ideal for making a versatile gluten-free flour. These nuts contain most of the minerals we require, albeit in small amounts, apart from iron and potassium, which are present here in useful amounts. Potassium is important to help regulate the fluid in our bodies and to keep blood pressure at a safe level. Chestnuts are also a good source of insoluble fiber, similar to that in grains, which helps to keep the digestive system working well and offers protection against heart disease.

- Lower in calories and fat than most nuts—ideal for those watching their weight and/or fat intake.
- A good source of vitamin C.
- Useful source of potassium for fluid regulation and healthier blood pressure.
- Useful source of insoluble fiber for heart and digestive health.

Practical tips:
Fresh chestnuts can be eaten raw, but they are usually cooked before eating. Roast (after cutting a cross in the top so that they don't explode in the oven) until tender or partly roast to make them easy to peel, then simmer in water or milk. Their starchiness makes them a good stuffing alternative to rice or bread crumbs. Use chestnut flour in place of cornstarch or wheat flour as a thickener for sauces and stews, or mix with other gluten-free flours to make an ideal flour for sweet baked goods, such as crepes and shortbreads.

DID YOU KNOW?

Sweet fresh chestnuts are the only nuts to supply vitamin C in good amounts—a small handful will give you around one-quarter of your RDA.

NUTRIENTS PER ⅓ CUP/1¾ OZ FRESH SHELLED CHESTNUTS

Calories	98
Protein	0.8 g
Fat	0.6 g
Carbohydrate	22 g
Fiber	2 g
Folate	29 mcg
Vitamin C	20 mg
Iron	0.5 mg
Potassium	242 mg

Squash and chestnut risotto

SERVES 4   ⓒ

1 tablespoon olive oil

3 tablespoons butter

1 small onion, finely chopped

2 cups diced butternut squash,
    acorn squash, or pumpkin

1½ cups cooked and shelled
    chestnuts

2 cups risotto rice

⅔ cup gluten-free dry white wine

1 teaspoon crumbled saffron
    threads (optional), dissolved in
    ¼ cup of the stock

4¼ cups simmering gluten-free
    vegetable stock

1 cup freshly grated Parmesan
    cheese, plus extra for serving

salt and pepper, to taste

Method

1 Heat the oil with 2 tablespoons of the butter in a deep, heavy saucepan over medium heat until the butter has melted. Stir in the onion and pumpkin and cook, stirring occasionally, for 5 minutes, or until the onion is soft and starting to turn golden and the pumpkin begins to brown.

2 Coarsely chop the chestnuts and add to the mixture. Stir thoroughly to coat.

3 Reduce the heat, add the rice, and mix to coat in oil and butter. Cook, stirring constantly, for 2–3 minutes, or until the grains are translucent. Add the wine and cook, stirring constantly, for 1 minute, until it has reduced.

4 Add the saffron liquid to the rice, if using, and cook, stirring constantly, until the liquid has been absorbed.

5 Gradually add the simmering stock, a ladleful at a time, stirring constantly. Add more liquid as the rice absorbs each addition. Increase the heat to medium so that the liquid is simmering.

6 Cook for 20 minutes, or until all the liquid has been absorbed and the rice is creamy. Season with salt and pepper.

7 Remove the risotto from the heat and add the remaining butter. Mix well, then stir in the Parmesan until it melts. Adjust the seasoning, if necessary.

8 Spoon the risotto onto four warm plates, sprinkle with grated Parmesan, and serve immediately.

30 BRAZIL NUTS

Rich in minerals, antioxidants, and healthy fats, Brazil nuts can boost your immune system and help protect against cancer.

Brazils contain a unique mix of fats—around 40 percent of their fat is monounsaturates, which help to boost HDL cholesterol, and around 35 percent polyunsaturates, which lowers LDL cholesterol. These super nuts are the highest of all foods in the antioxidant mineral selenium, which appears to protect us against cancers and other diseases of aging. Selenium levels in our staple foods have been dropping in recent decades as farming methods alter, so this nut is an easy way to boost your intake, especially in a gluten-free diet. But don't eat a lot in one go; see "Did you know?," left. The nuts also have good levels of magnesium, calcium, and phosphorous for healthy bones and a 4-nut/¾-ounce portion provides one-third of your RDA for vitamin E.

- High in unsaturated fats to improve blood lipids profile.
- Extremely rich in antioxidant, anticancer selenium.
- High in vitamin E, which boosts your immune system and helps protect skin.
- Rich in a range of important minerals.

Practical tips:
Because of their high polyunsaturated fat content, Brazils should be kept in cool, dark conditions and eaten within weeks to help prevent their fats from oxidizing (turning rancid). Eat raw to get more benefit from the healthy fats and vitamin E.

DID YOU KNOW?

While Brazil nuts are a healthy food, don't eat them all day long. At around 95 mcg selenium per nut, overeating them could give you selenium toxicity. Four nuts (¾ oz) will give you just under 400 mcg, which is the recommended upper daily limit.

NUTRIENTS PER 4 NUTS/¾ OZ FRESH SHELLED BRAZILS

Calories	131
Protein	2.8 g
Fat	13.3 g
Carbohydrate	2.4 g
Fiber	1.5 g
Vitamin E	2.9 mg
Calcium	32 mg
Iron	0.5 mg
Magnesium	75 mg
Phosphorous	145 mg
Potassium	132 mg
Selenium	383 mcg
Zinc	0.8 mg

Honey and spice snacking nuts

SERVES 6   Ⓕ Ⓟ Ⓝ

½ cup Brazil nuts
½ cup pecans
½ cup cashew nuts
2 tablespoons pumpkin seeds
1 tablespoon sunflower oil
1½ tablespoons honey
½ teaspoon ground cinnamon
½ teaspoon allspice
½ teaspoon black pepper
½ teaspoon sweet paprika
¼ teaspoon salt

Method

1 Line a baking sheet with parchment paper and preheat the oven to 275°F.
2 Combine all the ingredients in a bowl, except for 1½ teaspoons of the honey, and then spread out onto the prepared baking sheet.
3 Place onto the middle shelf of the oven and cook for 10 minutes. Remove from the oven and drizzle the remaining honey over the nuts. Let cool, then serve. Store in an airtight container for up to a week.

31 HAZELNUTS

Hazelnuts are a great food to eat for your cardiovascular health, because they contain several heart health-boosting nutrients.

Hazelnuts are high in the flavonoid group of plant chemicals, including quercetin and kaempferol, to support heart health. The nuts are also a source of several other beneficial plant compounds, including betaine, which helps clear the blood of harmful homocysteine, and phytosterols, which also help improve the blood fats profile by lowering cholesterol. The fats in hazelnuts have additional cholesterol-lowering effects—they are mostly monounsaturated and can reduce LDL cholesterol and raise "good" HDL cholesterol. Hazelnuts are also extremely high in vitamin E and magnesium, two antioxidants that maintain heart health, and in potassium for help in regulating blood pressure.

- High in flavonoids to promote heart health.
- Rich in plant compounds, which also support the cardiovascular system.
- Great source of vitamin E, magnesium, and potassium.
- Rich in monounsaturated fats to raise HDL cholesterol.

Practical tips:

Buy whole nuts instead of chopped—the chopping process destroys much of the nutrient content and shortens their shelf life. Use as a snack, breakfast, or dessert or add to salads and stir-fries. Hazelnut oil—at 120 calories per tablespoon—is even higher in monounsaturated fat than olive oil and makes an ideal salad dressing. Hazelnut flour or meal can be used in a wide variety of baking recipes (store it in the refrigerator or freezer).

DID YOU KNOW?

Hazelnuts are one of the few nuts native to the UK and still grow wild across the country, ripening in October. Other names for hazelnuts are filberts and cobnuts.

NUTRIENTS PER ⅓ CUP/1¾ OZ FRESH SHELLED HAZELNUTS

Calories	314
Protein	7.5 g
Fat	30.4 g
Carbohydrate	8.4 g
Fiber	4.8 g
Vitamin B_1	0.3 mg
Vitamin B_5	0.5 mg
Vitamin B_6	0.3 mg
Folate	57 mcg
Niacin	0.9 mg
Vitamin E	7.5 mg
Calcium	57 mg
Iron	2.4 mg
Magnesium	82 mg
Potassium	340 mg
Zinc	1.2 mg

Green tea and hazelnut ice cream

SERVES 6

1⅔ cups canned coconut milk

1 (7-ounce) box unsweetened creamed coconut (available from Asian grocery stores, gourmet food stores, online; or use 3 cups coconut cream and omit the coconut milk)

1 cup sugar

1 tablespoon green tea powder

½ cup roast hazelnuts, chopped

Method

1 Put the coconut milk and creamed coconut into a medium saucepan over medium heat. Stir continuously, until both ingredients have blended together. (Or heat the coconut cream.)

2 Whisk in the sugar and green tea powder. Stir in the chopped hazelnuts and set aside to cool to room temperature.

3 Transfer to an ice cream machine and churn according to the manufacturer's directions. Alternatively, pour the cooled mixture into a shallow, freezer-proof container and place in the freezer. Let freeze for about 1 hour, then remove from the freezer, stir, and freeze again until firm. Store in the freezer until required.

32

WALNUTS

A stand-out healthy food, walnuts are the only nut high in omega-3 fat and are also rich in a special form of vitamin E.

Walnuts are one of the few plant foods to contain a high level of the heart-protective, omega-3 fat alpha-linolenic acid—one of the fats essential in our diet. Unless we eat plenty of fish, it is easy to have a shortage of this important fat in your diet, so including walnuts in your diet will help boost your intake. These nuts are also high in gamma-tocopherol, a form of vitamin E that is the focus of much research because of its strong anti-inflammatory effects and its ability to significantly lower LDL cholesterol and reduce the risk of coronary heart disease and prostate cancer. Walnuts can also help with weight and diabetes control.

- One of the few plant foods rich in omega-3 fats.
- Unusual in its high content of anti-inflammatory vitamin E gamma-tocopherol.
- Can help with both weight loss and diabetes control.
- A good source of polyphenols, which protect the heart, the B vitamins, and most minerals.

Practical tips:

Walnuts may turn rancid in storage because they are rich in polyunsaturated fats, so buy whole kernels, store in the refrigerator, and chop as needed. Eat raw with skins on to get the most benefit from their oils, polyphenols, and vitamin E. Try them as a pesto with walnut oil and basil, or sprinkle over breakfast cereal or into a salad with blue cheese and pears, using a walnut oil dressing.

DID YOU KNOW?

Walnut oil not only tastes great but is one of our richest sources of the essential fat alpha-linolenic acid. Just one tablespoon provides 1.7 g—nearly a whole day's recommended amount.

NUTRIENTS PER ⅓ CUP/1¾ OZ FRESH SHELLED WALNUTS

Calories	327
Protein	7.6 g
Fat	32.6 g
Carbohydrate	6.9 g
Fiber	3.4 g
Vitamin B$_5$	0.3 mg
Vitamin B$_6$	0.3 mg
Folate	49 mcg
Niacin	0.6 mg
Vitamin E (gamma)	10.4 mg
Calcium	49 mg
Iron	1.5 mg
Magnesium	79 mg
Potassium	221 mg
Zinc	1.5 mg

Zucchini and walnut bread

MAKES 2 LOAVES　(c)

butter, for greasing
2¾ cups gluten-free
　all-purpose flour
1 teaspoon gluten-free baking
　powder
2 teaspoons xanthan gum
1 teaspoon gluten-free
　baking soda
1 teaspoon ground allspice
2 teaspoons ground cinnamon
1 cup sugar
3 eggs
1 cup vegetable oil
2 teaspoons vanilla extract
1 cup walnuts, coarsely chopped
2 cups shredded zucchini

Method

1　Preheat the oven to 325°F. Grease two 8½ x 4½ x 2½-inch loaf
　pans and line with parchment paper.

2　Sift together the flour, baking powder, xanthan gum, baking soda,
　and spices into a large bowl.

3　In a separate bowl, beat the sugar, eggs, vegetable oil, and vanilla
　extract to a creamy consistency. Add the flour mixture, walnuts,
　and zucchini to the bowl and fold in to make a smooth batter.

4　Divide the batter between the two pans and bake in the preheated
　oven for 55–60 minutes, until firm to the touch.

5　Let cool in the pans for 20 minutes before transferring to a wire
　rack to cool. Let the bread rest on the rack for at least 30 minutes
　before serving.

33

PISTACHIO NUTS

Pistachios contain several compounds and nutrients that help control diabetes, boost immunity, and reduce the risk of heart disease and eye problems.

NUTRIENTS PER ⅓ CUP/1¾ OZ FRESH SHELLED PISTACHIOS

Calories	281
Protein	10 g
Fat	22.7 g
Carbohydrate	13.8 g
Fiber	5.2 g
Vitamin A	62 mcg
Vitamin B₁	0.4 mg
Vitamin B₆	0.8 mg
Vitamin E	1 mg
Calcium	53 mg
Iron	2 mg
Magnesium	61 mg
Phosphorous	245 mg
Potassium	513 mg
Zinc	1.1 mg
Lutein/zeaxanthin	703 mcg
Beta-carotene	125 mcg

They are a particularly good source of fiber and protein, which gives them a low GI, and including them in your diet will help control diabetes. The nuts are also rich in a variety of compounds to help lower cholesterol and help prevent cardiovascular disease. These include beta-sitosterols and resveratrol, both of which may also protect against cancer. Pistachios are a great source of vitamins A and E for healthy skin, and vitamin B6, which helps in the production of hemoglobin to supply oxygen throughout our bodies and boost immunity. Their high content of the carotenes lutein and zeaxanthin means they are helpful in protecting our eyes from macular degeneration.

- Can help prevent or control type-2 diabetes.
- Contain cholesterol-lowering compounds beta-sitosterols and resveratrol.
- Contain plant compounds that also help prevent cancers.
- Immune-boosting and useful to help protect eyes.

Practical tips:
Pistachios are widely used in savory and sweet Italian, Middle Eastern, and Indian cuisine—from pilafs and pâtés to ice creams and cookies. They go well with pomegranate seeds and quinoa in a winter salad, add nutrients and color to a crumb stuffing, and are great in a nut roast. A handful makes a healthy snack.

Pistachio macarons

MAKES 24

½ cup skinned pistachio nuts,
 plus extra to decorate
⅓ cup confectioners' sugar
1 tablespoon rice flour
2 egg whites
¼ cup superfine sugar (or
 granulated sugar processed
 in a blender for 1 minute)
⅔ cup unsweetened
 dried coconut
1 tablespoon chopped fresh mint

Method

1 Preheat the oven to 350°F and line two baking sheets with
 parchment paper.
2 Put the pistachio nuts, confectioners' sugar, and rice flour into a
 food processor and process until finely ground.
3 Whisk the egg whites in a clean, dry bowl until stiff, then gradually
 whisk in the superfine sugar. Fold in the pistachio mixture, coconut,
 and mint.
4 Place spoonfuls of the batter onto the prepared baking sheets and
 press a pistachio on top of each to decorate.
5 Bake in the preheated oven for about 20 minutes, until firm and just
 beginning to brown. Let cool on the baking sheets and serve.

34 PEANUTS

Peanuts contain more plant sterols (good for lowering cholesterol) than other nuts and are rich in mood-boosting and heart-protective nutrients.

Peanuts are rich in phytosterols, which can lower cholesterol by up to 15 percent, and high in antioxidant polyphenols. These include resveratrol to protect the heart; coumaric acid, which may protect against stomach cancer; and isoflavones that protect against breast and prostate cancers. They are a good source of vitamin E, an antioxidant linked with heart and arterial health, and are extremely rich in niacin, the B vitamin that improves blood flow to the brain and helps release energy from food. They are also a great source of the mood-boosting amino acid, tryptophan.

- High in plant sterols, which can have a dramatic cholesterol-lowering effect.
- Rich in antioxidant compounds to protect the heart and fight cancers.
- High in vitamin E for arterial and skin health.
- Rich source of niacin and monounsaturated fats.

Practical tips:
Buy peanuts in their shells or at least in their skins—they will keep longer and retain more nutrients. They make a great snack sprinkled with a little smoked paprika and roasted, or try them in a carrot and cabbage coleslaw dressed with peanut oil. Roasting the nuts can increase antioxidant levels. Commercial peanut butters often contain sugar and salt, so try making your own—blend shelled peanuts in a blender with a little peanut oil until you have a good spreading consistency.

DID YOU KNOW?

Peanut oil is almost as high in healthy monounsaturates as olive oil and canola oil, and it also contains a small amount of the essential omega-3 fat, alpha-linolenic acid. Peanut oil has a high smoke point, making it ideal for sautéing.

NUTRIENTS PER ⅓ CUP/1¾ OZ FRESH SHELLED PEANUTS

Calories	284
Protein	12.9 g
Fat	24.6 g
Carbohydrate	8 g
Fiber	4.3 g
Folate	120 mcg
Niacin	6 mg
Vitamin E	4.1 mg
Calcium	46 mg
Iron	2.3 mg
Magnesium	84 mg
Potassium	353 mg
Zinc	1.6 mg

Chicken and spicy peanut salad

SERVES 4 (v) (n)

¼ cup chunky peanut butter

2 tablespoons lemon juice

1 garlic clove, finely chopped

1 tablespoon finely chopped
    fresh ginger

2 teaspoons sesame oil

1 tablespoon packed light
    brown sugar

1 tablespoon gluten-free tamari
    (Japanese soy sauce)

1 tablespoon water

¼ –½ teaspoon cayenne pepper

2 tablespoons finely chopped
    fresh cilantro

2 scallions, thinly sliced

⅔ head of romaine lettuce,
    chopped

1 cucumber, sliced

1 small red, yellow, or orange bell
    pepper, seeded and diced

2½ cups diced, cooked skinless,
    boneless chicken breast

Method

1 In a small bowl, combine the peanut butter, lemon juice, garlic, ginger, sesame oil, brown sugar, tamari, water, and cayenne. Stir in the cilantro and scallions.

2 In a large serving bowl, toss the lettuce, cucumber, and bell pepper with a few spoonfuls of the peanut dressing. Divide the salad among four serving plates or bowls. Top with the chicken, then drizzle with more of the dressing. Serve immediately.

35

CASHEW NUTS

Cashew nuts contain a good balance of protein, carbohydrates, and minerals, and they are rich in a type of oil that helps protect the heart.

Lower in fat than many other nuts, cashew nuts contain a good balance of nutrients and make the ideal low-GI food to eat as a snack to maintain steady blood sugar levels while boosting your carb intake. The fat in cashew nuts is mostly oleic acid—a monounsaturated fat that is linked with good cardiovascular health. Cashew nuts are high in magnesium, a mineral that works with calcium to promote healthy bones and teeth and can help to lower high blood pressure. They are higher in selenium, a mineral that may reduce the risk of cancer, than most other nuts and also contain useful amounts of immune-boosting zinc and fluid-regulating potassium.

- A good source of carbohydrates and protein.
- Rich in oleic acid, linked with heart and arterial protection.
- High in magnesium for healthy bones and teeth.
- Good source of selenium to lower the risk of cancer.

Practical tips:
Unsalted cashew nuts make a great addition to all kinds of recipes. Add a handful of lightly toasted cashew nuts to a vegetarian stir-fry or curry just before you serve to increase the protein content. Add them to hot or cold rice dishes to add crunch and nutrients. Pack some with sunflower seeds and golden raisins for a snack ideal for traveling. Store cashew nuts in the refrigerator to maintain the nutrient content, or you can even freeze them for up to a year.

DID YOU KNOW?

Cashew nuts are sold preshelled because the shells contain urushiol, a skin irritant (the kernels don't).

NUTRIENTS PER ⅓ CUP/1¾ OZ FRESH SHELLED CASHEW NUTS

Calories	277
Protein	9 g
Fat	22 g
Carbohydrate	15 g
Fiber	1.6 g
Vitamin B$_1$	0.2 mg
Vitamin B$_6$	0.2 mg
Niacin	0.5 mg
Iron	3.3 mg
Magnesium	146 mg
Phosphorous	297 mg
Potassium	330 mg
Selenium	10 mcg
Zinc	2.9 mg

Cashew nut and chickpea curry

SERVES 4 Ⓒ Ⓕ Ⓥ

1 large Yukon gold or red-
    skinned potato, chopped
    into bite-size pieces
3 tablespoons vegetable oil
1 onion, chopped
2 garlic cloves, chopped
1¼-inch piece fresh ginger,
    peeled and finely chopped
1 teaspoon cumin seeds
1 teaspoon chili powder
½ teaspoon ground turmeric
½ teaspoon ground cinnamon
1 (15-ounce) can chickpeas,
    drained and rinsed
1 cup cashew nuts
1 cup gluten-free
    vegetable stock
1 cup coconut milk
chopped fresh cilantro,
    to garnish
cooked rice, to serve

Method

1 Put the potato into a large saucepan of boiling water and cook
   for 10–15 minutes, until tender but still firm.
2 Heat the oil in a large saucepan over medium heat. Sauté the
   onion, garlic, ginger, cumin seeds, chili powder, turmeric, and
   cinnamon for 5 minutes, or until the onion is soft and translucent.
3 Stir in the boiled potato, chickpeas, and cashew nuts, and cook
   for an additional 3 minutes. Stir in the stock and coconut milk.
   Reduce the heat to low and continue to cook for 15 minutes,
   or until thick and creamy.
4 Garnish with cilantro and serve immediately with cooked rice.

36 PINE NUTS

Pine nuts are an important source of the omega-3 fat ALA and several other nutrients known for helping to keep your cardiovascular system healthy.

The small seeds are rich in polyunsaturated fat, much of which is in the form of omega-6s, but they also contain a small amount of the omega-3 essential fat, alpha-linolenic acid (ALA). This is one of the two "essential fats" that must be provided by diet because our bodies cannot make it. ALA can even convert in the body to EPA and DHA, the two unique fats found mainly in oily fish that promote a healthy cardiovascular system and reduce the pain of rheumatoid arthritis. Pine nuts are also high in vitamin E and zinc, two antioxidants to help the heart, boost the immune system, and increase fertility. And there are important plant sterols and stanols here—compounds that help lower blood cholesterol and boost the immune system.

• One of few plant foods to contain ALA in significant amounts.
• Helps to promote heart and arterial health.
• Contains immune-boosting antioxidants zinc and vitamin E.
• Helps minimize symptoms of arthritis.

Practical tips:
Pine nuts have a distinctive flavor and delicate texture. Try them in dishes cooked with broccoli, spinach, golden raisins, and oily fish. They are a traditional ingredient of Italian basil pesto and can be sprinkled over many pasta dishes. Because pine nuts are so rich in polyunsaturates, they turn rancid quickly, so store in the refrigerator and use within a month.

DID YOU KNOW?

Pine nuts come from several species of pine trees and are harvested in the Mediterranean, Asia, and even the United States. All have similar nutritional profiles.

NUTRIENTS PER 2 TABLESPOONS PINE NUTS

Calories	101
Protein	2 g
Fat	10.2 g
Carbohydrate	2 g
Fiber	0.6 g
Vitamin E	1.4 mg
Iron	0.8 mg
Magnesium	38 mg
Potassium	90 mg
Zinc	1 mg

Baby broccoli with pine nuts

SERVES 4 Ⓕ Ⓥ Ⓝ

1½ pounds baby broccoli
3 tablespoons extra virgin
   olive oil
3 shallots, thinly sliced
2 large garlic cloves, thinly sliced
pinch of crushed red
   pepper flakes
3 tablespoons pine nuts, toasted
4 tablespoons butter
2 tablespoons capers, drained
¼ cup snipped fresh chives
1 ounce Parmesan cheese,
   shaved into wafers
sea salt and pepper, to taste

Method

1 Cut off the broccoli florets and slice lengthwise if thick. Slice the leaves and stems into ¾-inch pieces. Steam for 2 minutes over a saucepan of boiling water, until barely soft. Remove from the heat. Reserve the cooking water.

2 Heat the oil in a large skillet over medium-low heat. Add the shallots and sauté for 5 minutes.

3 Add the garlic and sauté for 2–3 minutes, until just starting to brown.

4 Increase the heat to medium and add the broccoli. Add the red pepper flakes and season with salt and pepper. Add 3–4 tablespoons of the broccoli cooking water. Cook, stirring, for 4–6 minutes, until the broccoli is just tender and still bright green.

5 Stir in the pine nuts and check the seasoning. Transfer to a serving dish and keep warm.

6 Heat a heavy skillet. When it is hot, add the butter and sizzle until golden.

7 Remove from the heat and stir in the capers and half the chives.

8 Pour the sauce over the broccoli. Sprinkle with the cheese shavings and the remaining chives.

37

PUMPKIN SEEDS

Pumpkin seeds have an unusual balance of omega fats and high levels of vitamin E— essential for good health and important in minimizing the risk of several diseases.

It is not just the type of fat that we eat (saturated, mono-, or polyunsaturated) that is important for disease prevention but the ratio of omega-6s and omega-3s (two types of polyunsaturates). Many people have much more omega-6 than is healthy and too little omega-3. Pumpkin seed oil has an almost perfect ratio of 3:1. The seeds are also one of the few plant foods to contain a significant amount of vitamin E in the form of gamma-tocopherol, which is strongly anti-inflammatory and is linked to a reduction in the risk of some cancers and heart disease. Pumpkin seeds are also high in plant sterols that can lower LDL cholesterol, raise HDL, and reduce blood pressure.

- Perfect balance of omega-6 and omega-3 fats to protect from disease.
- High in anti-inflammatory vitamin E gamma-tocopherol for additional disease protection.
- Rich in several minerals, including zinc and magnesium.
- Contain plant sterols to lower LDL and raise HDL cholesterol.

Practical tips:
Pumpkin seeds are almost always sold with the outer pale shell removed although it is perfectly edible. Add the seeds to store-bought muesli or granola or eat mixed with chopped fruit and yogurt. Try them lightly roasted in the oven as a snack or sprinkle them over salads. Grind or chop the seeds and add to a veggie burger mix. Use pumpkin seed oil in salad dressings or drizzled over a nut roast.

DID YOU KNOW?

Make your own: You can dry the seeds from the center of any pumpkin or squash and then roast them gently on a low heat for about 20 minutes or so.

NUTRIENTS PER 2½ TABLESPOONS PUMPKIN SEEDS

Calories	168
Protein	9 g
Fat	14.7 g
Carbohydrate	3.2 g
Fiber	1.8 g
Niacin	1.5 mg
Vitamin E (gamma)	10.5 mg
Iron	2.6 mg
Magnesium	178 mg
Phosphorous	170 mg
Potassium	243 mg
Zinc	2.3 mg

Indian spiced slaw

SERVES 4 (F)(V)(D)(N)

2 cups shredded red cabbage
⅔ cup shredded kale
1 red apple, such as Red
    Delicious, cored and
    coarsely grated
1 large carrot, shredded

Topping

2 tablespoons pumpkin seeds
2 tablespoons sunflower seeds
2 tablespoons slivered almonds
½ teaspoon gluten-free garam
    masala
¼ teaspoon ground turmeric
1 tablespoon sunflower oil

Dressing

⅔ cup plain yogurt
1 teaspoon gluten-free garam
    masala
¼ teaspoon ground turmeric
salt and pepper, to taste

Method

1 To make the topping, preheat a skillet over medium heat. Put
    the pumpkin seeds, sunflower seeds, almonds, garam masala,
    and turmeric in the hot pan and pour the oil over them. Cook for
    3–4 minutes, stirring often, until the almonds are golden brown.
    Let cool.

2 To make the dressing, put the yogurt, garam masala, and
    turmeric in a large bowl, then season with salt and pepper and
    stir well.

3 Add the cabbage, kale, apple, and carrot to the bowl and toss
    gently together. Divide the salad among four bowls, sprinkle the
    topping over the salad, and serve.

38

SESAME SEEDS

Even in small amounts, tiny sesame seeds can offer a boost to your nutrient intake. They are rich in important fibers, minerals, and plant sterols.

The fiber content of sesame seeds is unusual because it is high in sesamin and sesamolin, two members of the lignan group of fibers that both lower LDL and blood pressure and can enhance the effect of vitamin E in the diet. The rich sterol content of the seeds also enhances the cholesterol-lowering effect. The seeds contain a good range of minerals and are high in bone-boosting calcium. They also have a high copper content—an anti-inflammatory mineral linked with protection from the symptoms of arthritis. Tahini is a ground sesame seed paste rich in all the nutrients contained in the seeds and sesame seed oil contains a good balance of monounsaturated and polyunsaturated fats.

- Contains special types of fiber that boost cardiovascular health.
- Rich in antioxidant vitamin E.
- High in copper, which can help reduce arthritic symptoms.
- Good source of calcium.

Practical tips:
Sprinkle the seeds on vegetables, such as broccoli or spinach, before serving or add to grain salads. Grind the seeds beforehand to help the body absorb the nutrients more easily. Tahini is an essential ingredient of the popular Middle Eastern purees baba ganoush and hummus. Try mixing extra tahini into hummus to enhance the flavor of the dip. Use sesame oil for stir-frying or, to get the most from its distinctive flavor, sprinkle a little on food before serving.

DID YOU KNOW?

Cold-pressed sesame oil makes an excellent healthy choice for salads, because it contains more vitamin E and nutrients than oils from other extraction methods. It is also less likely to oxidize when fried at high temperatures, so is ideal for stir-fries.

NUTRIENTS PER 1½ TABLESPOONS SESAME SEEDS

Calories	86
Protein	2.6 g
Fat	7.5 g
Carbohydrate	3.5 g
Fiber	1.8 g
Calcium	146 mg
Iron	2.2 mg
Magnesium	53 mg
Potassium	70 mg
Zinc	1.2 mg

Toffee bananas

SERVES 4   (C) (F)

½ cup gluten-free
　all-purpose flour
½ teaspoon gluten-free
　baking powder
1 egg, beaten
⅓ cup ice water
4 large, ripe bananas
3 tablespoons lemon juice
2 tablespoons rice flour
vegetable oil, for deep-frying

Toffee

⅔ cup sugar
¼ cup ice water, plus an extra
　bowl of ice water for setting
2 tablespoons sesame seeds

Method

1　Sift the flour and baking powder into a bowl. Make a well in the center, add the egg and ice water, and whisk to a smooth batter.

2　Peel the bananas and cut into 2-inch pieces. Gently shape them into balls with your hands. Brush with lemon juice to prevent discoloration, then roll in rice flour to coat. Pour the oil into a saucepan to a depth of 2½ inches and preheat to 375°F, or until a cube of bread browns in 30 seconds. Coat the bananas in the batter and cook, in batches, in the hot oil for about 2 minutes each, until golden. Lift them out and drain on paper towels.

3　To make the toffee, put the sugar into a small saucepan over low heat. Add the water and heat, stirring, until the sugar dissolves. Simmer for 5 minutes, remove from the heat, and stir in the sesame seeds. Toss the banana balls in the toffee, scoop them out, and drop into the bowl of ice water to set. Lift them out and divide among individual serving bowls. Serve hot.

39

SUNFLOWER SEEDS

Sunflower seeds are packed with important nutrients that are often lacking in a gluten-free diet, which offer protection against several major diseases.

These seeds are one of the richest in vitamin E. Natural vitamin E (instead of in supplement form) is a valuable antioxidant, protecting us from the diseases of aging, including cardiovascular disease, cancers, and arthritis. One 10-teaspoon portion of sunflower seeds gives you around two-thirds of your RDA. It also provides one-quarter of your selenium RDA to protect against cancer and one-quarter of your vitamin B6. This vitamin helps clear the blood of homocysteine, high levels of which contribute to heart disease. The seeds are particularly rich in cholesterol-lowering plant sterols, and sunflower oil is a major source of the essential omega-6 fat, linoleic acid.

- Rich in vitamins B1 and E, and selenium, all of which may be low in the average gluten-free diet.
- Offer protection from cardiovascular disease, arthritis, and cancer.
- High in plant sterols to lower cholesterol.
- An excellent source of vitamin B6, niacin, folate, magnesium, and zinc.

Practical tips:
Store sunflower seeds in a cool, dry, dark place in an airtight container and eat within three months, because their high polyunsaturates content makes them vulnerable to spoiling. Add the seeds to breakfast cereals and salads, or to a nut, seed, and dried fruit mix to boost nutrient content. Virgin sunflower oil is delicious in a salad dressing or mixed with olive oil to make a mayonnaise.

DID YOU KNOW?

If you use refined sunflower oil for high-temperature cooking, don't save it and reuse it, because frequent reheating of omega-6 oils produces toxins that may damage your health.

NUTRIENTS PER 10 TEASPOONS SUNFLOWER SEEDS

Calories	175
Protein	6.2 g
Fat	15.4 g
Carbohydrate	6 g
Fiber	2.6 g
Vitamin B6	0.4 mg
Folate	68 mcg
Niacin	2.5 mg
Vitamin E	10.5 mg
Calcium	23 mg
Iron	1.6 mg
Magnesium	98 mg
Potassium	194 mg
Selenium	16 mcg
Zinc	1.5 mg

Apple and seed muesli

MAKES 10 SERVINGS   (C)(F)(V)(D)(N)

½ cup sunflower seeds

¼ cup pumpkin seeds

¾ cup coarsely chopped
    hazelnuts

2¾ cups buckwheat flakes

2½ cups rice flakes

1¼ cups millet flakes

1⅓ cups coarsely chopped
    dried apple

¾ cup coarsely chopped,
    dried pitted dates

Method

1 Heat a nonstick skillet over medium heat. Add the seeds
   and hazelnuts and lightly toast, shaking the pan frequently, for
   4 minutes, or until golden brown. Transfer to a large bowl and
   let cool.

2 Add the flakes, apple, and dates to the bowl and mix thoroughly
   until combined. Store the muesli in an airtight jar or container.

40

FLAXSEED

Tiny flaxseed have an almost unique fat profile with a remarkably high level of beneficial omega-3 fats.

Flaxseed are the richest of all commonly eaten plant foods in the essential fat alpha-linolenic acid (ALA), one of the omega-3 fats that experts say we should get more of in our diets. More than 50 percent of the oil in flaxseed is ALA. The seeds are a useful food for vegetarians because the ALA converts to the fats EPA and DHA in the body—these are the special long-chain fats found in oily fish and are both anti-inflammatory and protect against cardiovascular disease. Some research shows that the omega-3 fats can also improve memory and help prevent depression and breast cancer. The seeds contain good amounts of soluble and insoluble fiber so are a good digestive aid. Cold-pressed flaxseed oil contains all the beneficial compounds found in the seeds in an easily digested form.

- Highest of all plant foods in omega-3 fats.
- Anti-inflammatory and protects against cardiovascular disease.
- May help improve memory, ease depression, and reduce the risk of breast cancer.
- Fiber content helps digestion.

Practical tips:
Store the seeds in a cool, dark, dry place to keep them fresh and use within a month. The nutrients and oils are harder to digest from whole seeds so it is a good idea to grind them before use. Add ground seeds to your breakfast cereal or yogurt, or sprinkle onto salads and into casseroles and vegetable dishes before serving. And use a little of the oil in salad dressings or sprinkled on steamed vegetables. Do not use the oil for cooking.

DID YOU KNOW?

You need only 2 tablespoons of flaxseed or their oil per day to see a reduction in LDL cholesterol, but because it has a low smoke point, don't use the oil for cooking.

NUTRIENTS PER 1½ TABLESPOONS FLAXSEED

Calories	80
Protein	2.7 g
Fat	6.3 g
Carbohydrate	4.3 g
Fiber	4.1 g
Calcium	38 mg
Iron	0.9 mg
Magnesium	59 mg
Potassium	122 mg
Zinc	0.6 mg

Three-seed salad

SERVES 4   (F) (V) (D) (N)

4 cups baby spinach
½ oakleaf lettuce, leaves
separated and torn into
bite-size pieces
2 celery stalks, sliced
small handful of celery leaves,
coarsely chopped, plus a few
extra to garnish
1 cup blueberries
juice of 1 lemon
salt and pepper, to taste

Dressing

2 tablespoons sesame seeds,
toasted, plus a few extra
to garnish
2 tablespoons sunflower seeds
2 tablespoons flaxseed
1 garlic clove, sliced
2 tablespoons olive oil
juice of 1 lemon
⅔ cup low-fat plain yogurt
salt and pepper, to taste

Method

1   Put the spinach and lettuce in a salad bowl. Sprinkle the celery, celery leaves, and blueberries over the greens. Drizzle with the lemon juice, season with salt and pepper, and toss gently together.

2   To make the dressing, put the sesame seeds, sunflower seeds, and flaxseed in a blender. Add the garlic, olive oil, and the lemon juice and season with salt and pepper. Process until the seeds are finely ground, then scrape from the sides and add the yogurt. Process again briefly until you have a fine paste.

3   Divide the salad among four plates and add a generous spoonful of the dressing to the center of each plate. Garnish with a few extra sesame seeds and celery leaves and serve.

41

EXTRA VIRGIN OLIVE OIL

Olive oil is the highest of all commonly eaten foods in monounsaturated fats, which have several potential health benefits.

Nearly three-quarters of the fat in olive oil is monounsaturated and over recent years several health benefits have been associated with this type of oil. Similarly to polyunsaturates, it can help lower LDL cholesterol, but it can also raise HDL cholesterol and offer even more protection against arterial and heart disease. The cold-pressed olive oils contain several plant compounds, including sterols and polyphenols, which increase this heart protective effect, and others that may reduce the risk of cancers and even minimize the symptoms of arthritis and reduce pain. Olive oil also contains a good amount of the antioxidant vitamin E for the immune system, healthy eyes, and skin.

- High in monounsaturated fat to improve the blood cholesterol profile.
- Cold-pressed oils contain a variety of sterols and plant compounds to protect the heart.
- High in vitamin E.
- Cold-pressed oils can help protect against some cancers and arthritic pain.

Practical tips:
Store olive oil in the dark and use within a few weeks. Try to buy cold-pressed olive oil because it will contain much higher levels of healthy plant compounds. Use olive oil in salad dressings, as a dip, or sprinkled over vegetables as a garnish. Use it instead of other fats for mashed potatoes and vegetable purees.

DID YOU KNOW?

Light and heat both deprive olive oil of its beneficial compounds. Avoid cooking with cold-pressed and extra virgin olive oil at high temperatures (over 375°F) because the beneficial compounds start to degrade around this point and can produce harmful free radicals.

NUTRIENTS PER 1 TABLESPOON EXTRA VIRGIN OLIVE OIL

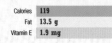

Calories	119
Fat	13.5 g
Vitamin E	1.9 mg

Olive oil-roasted vegetables

SERVES 4   (F)(V)(D)(N)

3 red bell peppers

1 cup olive oil

1 zucchini, thickly sliced

1 fennel bulb, coarsely chopped

2 large red onions, coarsely sliced

3 white onions, thickly sliced

2 extra-large eggplants,
   thickly sliced

5 ripe tomatoes, blanched,
   peeled, cored, and seeded

1 tablespoon fresh
   thyme leaves

1 tablespoon fresh
   rosemary leaves

1 teaspoon sugar

salt and pepper, to taste

Method

1 Preheat the broiler to high, then put the red bell peppers on the broiler pan and broil until the skins blacken. Turn and broil again, continuing until they are blackened all over. Put them in a bowl and cover with plastic wrap to sweat for about 10 minutes, then peel off the skin under cold running water. Cut them open and seed them, then chop the flesh into large chunks.

2 Meanwhile, put a large, heavy saucepan over medium heat and add half of the oil. Add the zucchini and cook until they begin to brown. Transfer to a large roasting pan and keep warm. Add the fennel and onions to the pan and sauté for 15–20 minutes, until they soften, then transfer them to the roasting pan. Add the eggplants and some more oil (they will soak up a lot) to the pan and sauté until they begin to brown. Add them to the roasting pan, laid flat in a single layer.

3 Preheat the oven to 375°F. Add the tomatoes, red bell peppers, thyme, and rosemary to the roasting pan. Sprinkle the sugar over the vegetables and mix through. There should be a tight layer of vegetables, not a stew. If you need more room, use two roasting pans. Season with salt and pepper, drizzle with the remaining olive oil, and place, uncovered, in the preheated oven for 40–50 minutes.

4 Eat immediately or let cool and eat cold.

42

CANOLA OIL

Canola oil has a particularly healthy balance of fats for heart health and is probably the best choice of oil for a wide range of culinary uses.

Canola oil is a good source of monounsaturated fats to lower LDL cholesterol and raise HDL, so lowering your risk of heart disease. It is also lower in saturates than olive oil and is the richest—at around 10 percent of its total fat content—of all the commonly used culinary oils in alpha-linolenic acid (ALA), an omega-3 essential fat that has been linked to heart health and is anti-inflammatory and immune-boosting, and improves insulin sensitivity. The oil has a high burning (smoke) point, which means it retains its health benefits and doesn't produce free radicals or carcinogens when used for high-temperature cooking. It is also low in trans fats and high in vitamin E, an antioxidant vitamin linked with healthy skin and protection against cardiovascular disease.

- Low in saturates and with a good balance of mono- and polyunsaturated fats.
- Higher than all other cooking oils in the essential omega-3 fat ALA.
- Good content of vitamin E.
- Extra virgin and cold-pressed types contain good levels of plant sterols.

Practical tips:
Cold-pressed or extra virgin canola oil is a healthy and tasty alternative to other oils in salads and as a dip. They also contain greater amounts of beneficial ALA, vitamin E, and compounds than refined canola oil.

DID YOU KNOW?

Canola oil is from an annual plant and a member of the brassica family. It has bright yellow flowers in summer and it is the seeds that are so rich in oil. Just 1 ½ tablespoons of canola oil per day will help boost your heart health.

NUTRIENTS
PER 1 TABLESPOON
CANOLA OIL

Calories	124
Fat	14 g
Vitamin E	2.4 mg

Summer potato salad

SERVES 4   © Ⓕ

1 pound new potatoes, skins on
5 scallions
1 good handful fresh mint leaves
1 good handful fresh parsley
¼ cup extra virgin canola oil
1 tablespoon white wine vinegar
1 teaspoon sugar
1 teaspoon gluten-free French-
   style mustard
salt and pepper, to taste

Method

1 Put the potatoes in a saucepan, cover with water, add a little salt, and place over medium-high heat. Bring to a boil and simmer for about 20 minutes, or until the potatoes are tender.

2 While the potatoes are cooking, slice the scallions, retaining most of the green parts, and finely chop the mint and parsley. In a bowl, mix together the oil, vinegar, sugar, mustard, and seasoning.

3 Drain the potatoes and return them in the pan to the hot stove (turned off) for 1 minute to evaporate any remaining moisture.

4 While the potatoes are still hot, transfer them to a bowl and coarsely chop them. Add the scallions, herbs, and dressing and stir to mix thoroughly. Cover and let stand for 1 hour to absorb the oil and flavorings before serving.

Fruits

Fruits, both fresh and dried, are invaluable because they add so much interest, flavor, and color to any diet. Most are high in vitamin C and potassium, while many are rich in carotenes that your body can convert to vitamin A. This important vitamin can be lacking in a gluten-free diet. Many fruits are also a good source of soluble fiber, which helps cardiovascular health, while their varied content of plant chemicals offers protection from many more diseases and health problems.

(C) High in carbohydrate
(F) Good source of fiber
(V) Rich in vitamins and minerals
(D) Particularly good for digestive health
(P) High in protein
(N) Nutrient boost for gluten-free diet

43

BANANAS

Bananas, with their high starch content and benefits for the digestive system, are a useful fruit to eat regularly on a gluten-free diet.

While bananas are not as high in vitamin C or antioxidants as some other fruits, they have plenty of other important nutrients. They are the only fruit high in starch instead of sugars; especially true if the banana is eaten before it becomes too ripe. This starch includes a type called "resistant starch," which ensures the fruit takes longer to be digested. This brings two main benefits: the fruit helps keep bowels regular, and it is also valuable in managing diabetes because blood sugar levels are less likely to fluctuate. This effect can also keep hunger pangs at bay. Bananas are rich in prebiotics, indigestible carbohydrates that feed probiotics (healthy bacteria) in the digestive system and keep the gut healthy. They are also rich in potassium for blood pressure and contain the amino acid tryptophan, which helps your body relax.

- Resistant starch content helps bowel regularity; prebiotics keep the digestive tract healthy.
- Can help keep blood sugar levels even—a great help in managing diabetes and hunger pangs.
- High potassium content helps control high blood pressure.
- Contains tryptophan, which promotes relaxation and sleep.

Practical tips:
While bananas are most often peeled and eaten raw, they can also be cooked. Bake in their skins or broil and serve with maple syrup. Ripe bananas make a delicious ingredient in cakes, muffins, and breads—mash and replace some of the sugar with the fruit. Mash ripe bananas and freeze as they are, or use in ice cream or sorbet.

DID YOU KNOW?

Because they have a short shelf life, bananas have been widely eaten across the world only since the twentieth century, after improvements in transport and the advent of refrigeration.

NUTRIENTS PER MEDIUM BANANA (3½ oz EDIBLE PORTION)

Calories	90
Protein	1 g
Fat	0.3 g
Carbohydrate	23 g
Fiber	2.6 g
Vitamin B$_6$	0.4 mg
Folate	10 mcg
Vitamin C	9 mg
Magnesium	27 mg
Potassium	362 mg

Banana crepes

SERVES 4 (C) (F) (D)

½ cup buckwheat flour
½ cup gluten-free
   all-purpose flour
pinch of salt
1 extra-large egg, lightly beaten
½ cup milk
½ cup water
3 tablespoons butter or
   margarine

Maple syrup bananas

3 tablespoons butter or
   margarine
2 tablespoons maple syrup
2 bananas, thickly sliced on the
   diagonal

Method

1 Sift the flours and the salt into a mixing bowl. Make a well in the center and add the beaten egg, milk, and water. Using a wire whisk, gradually mix the flour into the liquid ingredients. Whisk until you have a smooth batter.

2 Melt 2 tablespoons of the butter in a small saucepan and stir it into the batter. Cover the batter and let rest for 30 minutes.

3 Melt half the remaining butter in a medium skillet. When the pan is hot, pour in enough batter to make a thin crepe, swirling the pan to achieve an even layer.

4 Cook one side until lightly browned, then, using a spatula, turn over and cook the other side. Slide onto a warm plate and cover with aluminum foil while you cook the remaining crepes, adding more butter when needed.

5 To make the maple syrup bananas, wipe the skillet, add the butter, and heat until melted. Stir in the maple syrup, then add the bananas and cook for 2–3 minutes, or until the bananas have just softened and the sauce has thickened and caramelized. To serve, fold the crepes in half and half again, then top with the bananas.

44 GRAPEFRUIT

The tart sweetness of fresh grapefruit makes them popular breakfast fruits, but their high soluble fiber content also means they're particularly good for anyone with bowel problems.

Of all fruits, grapefruit is one of the richest in vitamin C—just one fruit contains our whole daily requirement. Vitamin C is a powerful anti-inflammatory antioxidant and can help slow the progress of arthritis as well as helping to prevent cardiovascular disease. It is also linked with improved mood, memory, and concentration. Fortunately, grapefruit is also rich in bioflavonoids, which enhance the effects of the vitamin C. Sweet, pink-fleshed grapefruit is a good source of lycopene, the carotene pigment that helps fight cancer and signs of aging, as well as three other cancer-fighting compounds: limonoids, glucarates, and naringenin. The fruits are high in the soluble fiber pectin and have a low GI, making them ideal for diabetics and weight control.

- High in vitamin C for a variety of health protection benefits.
- May help boost mood and memory.
- Rich in plant compounds that protect against cancers.
- Ideal fruit for weight-loss plans and diabetics.

Practical tips:
Make sure the grapefruit is fully ripe before eating, because it will then contain the maximum amount of antioxidants—a ripe grapefruit should feel plump and heavy. The easiest way to eat grapefruit is to halve, cut into the segments, and spoon out the flesh, but grapefruit pieces are delicious added to salads and salsas. The white pith is also high in beneficial compounds.

DID YOU KNOW?

Anyone on medication should check with their doctor that it is safe to consume grapefruit—the juice can alter the effect of certain medications, including some that lower blood pressure and cholesterol.

NUTRIENTS PER HALF MEDIUM PINK GRAPEFRUIT

Calories	30
Protein	0.5 g
Fat	Trace
Carbohydrate	7.5 g
Fiber	1.1 g
Folate	9 mcg
Vitamin C	37 mg
Calcium	15 mg
Potassium	127 mg
Beta-carotene	770 mcg

Avocado, pineapple, and grapefruit salad

SERVES 4 (F)(V)(D)(N)

*2 pink grapefruits, peeled
with a knife and cut into
segments, membrane
reserved*

*½ pineapple, sliced, peeled,
cored, and diced*

*1 large avocado, halved, pitted,
peeled, and diced*

*finely grated zest and juice of
1 lime*

*2 tablespoons finely chopped
fresh mint*

4 outer iceberg lettuce leaves

Method

1 Halve each grapefruit segment, then put them in a salad bowl. Squeeze the juice from the membrane over the segments. Add the pineapple and avocado, sprinkle with the lime zest and juice and mint, then gently toss together.

2 Arrange a lettuce leaf on each of four small plates. Spoon salad into the center of each lettuce leaf and serve immediately.

45 ORANGES

Oranges are one of the best sources of vitamin C, the vital vitamin that boosts the immune system and protects us from the signs of aging, and they are packed with other useful nutrients.

Oranges are one of the least expensive fruit sources of vitamin C and are an important part of the diet during the winter, when vitamin C levels can dip. Vitamin C is an antioxidant, helping to protect us from cell damage, aging, and disease, as well as keeping the immune system functioning properly. Oranges are also a good source of folate, a B vitamin that can be lacking in a gluten-free diet, and potassium, and they are higher than most other fruits in calcium—vital for bone maintenance. They have an excellent pectin content, to help control cholesterol, and also contain rutin (a flavonoid that can help slow down or prevent the growth of tumors) and nobiletin, an anti-inflammatory compound.

- Increased vitamin C intake can lessen the severity and duration of colds.
- Flavonoid content protects against cancer and heart disease.
- Good content of pectin, a soluble fiber to protect the arteries.
- Anti-inflammatory—may help reduce incidence of arthritis.

Practical tips:
Store oranges in the refrigerator to retain the vitamin C content (avoid keeping them in a fruit bowl in a warm, light room). Eat some of the white "pith" of the orange with the orange flesh, because the pith contains higher amounts of fiber and more plant chemicals and antioxidants. The orange peel is also rich in nutrients, but it should be thoroughly scrubbed clean and dried before use.

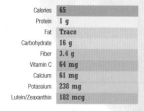

DID YOU KNOW?

To get the most juice from your orange, it needs to be warm. Bring it to room temperature before using, or put it in the microwave for 30 seconds.

NUTRIENTS PER MEDIUM ORANGE

Calories	65
Protein	1 g
Fat	Trace
Carbohydrate	16 g
Fiber	3.4 g
Vitamin C	64 mg
Calcium	61 mg
Potassium	238 mg
Lutein/Zeaxanthin	182 mcg

Broiled cinnamon oranges

SERVES 4   (F) (D) (N)

4 large oranges
1 teaspoon ground cinnamon
1 tablespoon raw brown sugar

Method

1 Preheat the broiler to high. Cut the oranges in half and discard any seeds. Using a sharp knife, carefully cut the flesh away from the skin by cutting around the edge of the fruit. Cut across the segments to loosen the flesh into bite-size pieces that will spoon out easily.

2 Arrange the orange halves, cut side up, in a shallow, flameproof dish. Mix the cinnamon with the sugar in a small bowl and sprinkle evenly over the orange halves.

3 Cook under the preheated broiler for 3–5 minutes, until the sugar has caramelized and is golden and bubbling. Serve immediately.

46

LEMONS

Indispensible in many recipes, lemons are rich in vitamin C for a wealth of health benefits, and they are packed with other disease-beating chemicals.

All parts of the lemon contain valuable nutrients and antioxidants. They are a particularly good source of vitamin C, while the plant compound antioxidants include limonene (an oil that may help to prevent breast and other types of cancer and may help to lower LDL blood cholesterol) and rutin, which has been found to strengthen veins and beat fluid retention. Lemons contain unique flavonoids called glucosides and kaempferol, which can help prevent many types of cancer from spreading. Lemons stimulate the taste buds and may be useful in dishes for people with a poor appetite.

- Rutin content may help to strengthen veins and prevent fluid retention.
- Flavonoids and limonenes can help to prevent or minimize breast and other cancers.
- Rich in vitamin C to combat arthritis and heart disease.
- Has disinfecting and insecticide properties.

Practical tips:
You can get more juice from a lemon if you warm it slightly (a few seconds in the microwave or in hot water) before squeezing. Always buy unwaxed organic lemons if you want to use the zest. Use lemon juice instead of vinegar in salad dressings or add a squeeze to mayonnaise. The acid and the antioxidants in lemon juice mean that it can help prevent foods, such as apples and avocados, from browning once peeled or cut. The acid also helps tenderize meat so the juice is great in marinades.

DID YOU KNOW?

The level of antioxidants in lemons increases as the fruit ripens, with the highest levels found when the fruit is just on the point of turning overripe and spoiling.

NUTRIENTS PER MEDIUM LEMON

Calories	17
Protein	0.6 g
Fat	Trace
Carbohydrate	5.4 g
Fiber	1.6 g
Vitamin C	31 mg
Potassium	80 mg

Honey and lemon corn muffins

MAKES 12 MUFFINS Ⓒ

*1 cup gluten-free
all-purpose flour*
¾ cup cornmeal
¼ cup sugar
*2 teaspoons gluten-free
baking powder*
¼ teaspoon xanthan gum
1 egg
juice and zest of ½ lemon
¼ cup vegetable oil
1 cup milk
2 tablespoons honey
1 tablespoon glycerin

Method

1 Preheat the oven to 350°F. Place 12 muffin cups in the sections of a deep muffin pan.

2 Put the flour, cornmeal, sugar, baking powder, and xanthan gum into a large bowl and mix together well.

3 In a separate bowl, mix together all the remaining ingredients. Add the liquid mixture to the dry mixture and fold in gently.

4 Spoon the batter into the muffin cups and bake them in the preheated oven for 18–20 minutes, until well risen and golden. Remove from the oven and let cool on a wire rack.

47

APPLES

Apples are one of the most popular fruits in the world and provide us with a range of nutrients, including soluble fiber, which may help calm a sensitive digestive tract.

Compared with many other fruits, apples aren't rich in vitamins, but they do contain a good range of plant chemicals. These include quercetin (a flavonoid with anticancer and anti-inflammatory properties that may protect against Alzheimer's disease) and anthocyanins for boosting memory. The peel contains ursolic acid, a compound that appears to help maintain muscle bulk and help prevent weight gain, as well as helping to lower cholesterol. Apples are also a valuable source of pectin, a type of soluble fiber that can help lower LDL cholesterol, protect the heart and circulation, and help prevent colon cancer. These low-GI fruits also help keep hunger at bay by releasing the hormone GLP-1, which sends "I'm full" signals to the brain.

- Rich in plant chemicals for a range of health benefits.
- High soluble fiber content can improve the blood lipids profile and reduce LDL cholesterol.
- A low-GI food, ideal for anyone watching their weight.

Practical tips:
Apple skin contains up to five times more plant chemicals than the flesh, so whenever possible eat the skin (wash first and/or buy organic) and choose red-skinned apples, which contain more beneficial compounds. When slicing apples, put the slices into a bowl of water with the juice of a lemon to prevent the flesh from browning (oxidizing). Eat a raw, whole apple when you can—they retain more nutrients than cooked or juiced apple.

....

DID YOU KNOW?

Adults who regularly eat apples have smaller waistlines, less abdominal fat, and lower blood pressure than those who don't. If making a dish with cooking apples, add cinnamon, which reduces the amount of sugar you need to add.

....

NUTRIENTS PER MEDIUM APPLE (4 oz)

Calories	60
Protein	Trace
Fat	Trace
Carbohydrate	16 g
Fiber	2.8 g
Vitamin C	5 mg
Potassium	123 mg

Apple and plum crisp

SERVES 4   ⒸⒻⒹ

4 apples, peeled, cored,
   and diced
5 plums, halved, pitted,
   and quartered
¼ cup fresh apple juice
2 tablespoons packed
   light brown sugar

Topping
1 cup gluten-free
   all-purpose flour
4 tablespoons butter, diced
½ cup buckwheat flakes
½ cup rice flakes
2½ tablespoons sunflower seeds
¼ cup firmly packed
   light brown sugar
¼ teaspoon ground cinnamon

Method

1 Preheat the oven to 350°F. Mix together the apples, plums, apple juice, and sugar in a 9-inch round pie dish.

2 To make the topping, sift the flour into a mixing bowl and rub in the butter with your fingertips until the mixture resembles coarse bread crumbs. Stir in the buckwheat and rice flakes, sunflower seeds, sugar, and cinnamon, then spoon the crumb topping over the fruit in the dish.

3 Bake the dessert in the preheated oven for 30–35 minutes, or until the topping is lightly browned and crisp.

48 PEARS

Pears are a particularly useful winter fruit, because they store well and are tasty cooked or raw. They are an ideal fruit for anyone with a sensitive digestive system.

Pears contain hydroxycinnamic acids—antioxidants that are anticancer and antibacterial and may help prevent gastroenteritis. They are also high in the soothing, soluble fiber pectin and have the lowest recorded rate of any fruit in provoking allergic reactions. This makes the fruit supremely useful for anyone who has a sensitive digestive system. They are also rich in flavonoids, which are not only anti-inflammatory but can also improve insulin sensitivity and help protect against type-2 diabetes. With a useful vitamin C and potassium content, they are an excellent food for all the family and are one of the few fruits recommended for young infants.

- Safe fruit for most children and people who experience food allergies and have a sensitive digestive tract.
- A good source of a range of nutrients, including vitamin C and potassium.
- Contains several plant chemicals, including antibacterial hydroxycinnamic acids and anti-inflammatory flavonoids.
- Can help protect against type-2 diabetes.

Practical tips:
Much of the fiber in pears is in the skin, so it is best to simply wash the fruit and not peel it unless absolutely necessary. Pears tend to brown easily once cut open—sprinkle the cut sides with lemon juice to prevent this. An ideal snack or lunch-bag fruit, pears are also versatile—they can be baked, sautéed, or poached, used in mixed fruit compotes or crisps, tarts, and pies.

DID YOU KNOW?

Pear cultivation began in Western Asia and dates back at least 3,000 years. There is even some evidence of pears being grown as long ago as the early Stone Age.

NUTRIENTS PER MEDIUM PEAR
(5½ oz)

Calories	86
Protein	0.6 g
Fat	Trace
Carbohydrate	23 g
Fiber	4.6 g
Vitamin C	6.2 mg
Potassium	176 mg

Pear, celery, blue cheese, and walnut salad

SERVES 4 (F) (V) (D) (N)

4 celery stalks

1 large, juicy red-skinned pear

a little lemon juice

3 tablespoons chopped fresh
    flat-leaf parsley

6 cups dark green salad greens,
    such as arugula, watercress,
    or baby spinach

4 ounces blue cheese, broken
    into small chunks

¼ cup coarsely chopped walnuts

sea salt flakes

Dressing

1 large, juicy pear

1 tablespoon lemon juice

¼ cup walnut oil

¼ teaspoon black pepper

sea salt flakes

Method

1 Trim the celery and remove the strings with a swivel peeler. Slice into bite-size pieces. Put into a shallow bowl.

2 Quarter and core the pear but do not peel. Slice each quarter lengthwise into thin segments. Add to the celery. Sprinkle with a little lemon juice to prevent discoloration.

3 To make the dressing, quarter and core the pear. Slice one quarter lengthwise into thin segments. Add to the pears in the bowl. Peel and coarsely chop the remaining pear quarters.

4 Process the chopped pear with the remaining dressing ingredients with a handheld immersion blender. Process for 30 seconds, until smooth. Scrape into a small bowl.

5 Toss the celery and pears with about ⅓ cup of the dressing, or enough to just coat. Stir in the parsley. Season with a little salt.

6 Arrange the salad greens on individual plates. Pile the pear and celery mixture attractively on top. Sprinkle with the cheese and nuts. Spoon the remaining dressing over the salad and serve.

49 GRAPES

Grapes are rich in polyphenols, compounds that protect the heart and circulation and help lower cholesterol. They are high in calories so are useful in a gluten-free diet.

Most of the beneficial compounds are in grape skins. Black, purple, and red varieties contain much higher levels of the dark pigments (anthocyanins) and the flavonoid quercetin than green grapes. Both of these may help prevent heart and cardiovascular disease and cancer. Two more compounds in grapes—resveratrol and tannins—have been linked to the prevention or inhibition of cancer and heart disease, degenerative nerve disease, viral infections, and Alzheimer's disease. With their relatively high sugar content, grapes are higher in carbohydrate and calories than many other fruits, and so they can be a useful source of carbs in a gluten-free diet. Raisins and golden raisins (dried grapes) are a concentrated form of the fruit with a high carb and good iron content but little vitamin C.

- Rich source of a variety of plant compounds.
- Help to prevent cancer.
- Encourage a healthy cardiovascular system, improve blood cholesterol, and have antiblood-clotting effect.
- Antiviral and antifungal action.

Practical tips:
Wash grapes before use, unless organic, because they may be sprayed with pesticides. Store uncovered in the refrigerator or a cool room to preserve vitamin C. Slice grapes for fruit salad at the last minute to prevent oxidation (loss of vitamin C and browning). Grapes are delicous raw but can also be used for making juice, jellies, vinegar, and sauces to accompany fish and chicken.

DID YOU KNOW?

Grapes can be frozen. Wash and dry them individually and place on a tray covered in robust paper towels. Freeze on the tray, then bag them.

NUTRIENTS PER AVERAGE SERVING
(⅔ cup/3½ oz)

Calories	70
Protein	0.7 g
Fat	Trace
Carbohydrate	18 g
Fiber	0.9 g
Vitamin C	10.8 mg
Calcium	14 mg
Potassium	191 mg

Quinoa, grape, and almond salad

SERVES 2 (C) (F) (V) (D) (P) (N)

¾ cup white quinoa, rinsed

1¼ cups water

½ teaspoon salt

1½ teaspoons lemon juice

1½ teaspoons gluten-free tamari
(Japanese soy sauce)

1½ teaspoons toasted sesame
oil, plus extra for drizzling

1⅓ cups snow peas

1 cup seedless black grapes,
halved

2 tablespoons almonds,
halved lengthwise

3 tablespoons snipped
fresh chives

2 small butterhead lettuce,
leaves separated

white pepper

Method

1 Put the quinoa into a saucepan with the water and salt. Bring to a boil, then reduce the heat, cover, and simmer for 15 minutes, or according to package directions. Remove from the heat, but keep the pan covered for an additional 5 minutes to let the grains swell. Fluff up with a fork and set aside.

2 Whisk together the lemon juice, tamari, sesame oil, and a little white pepper. Pour the dressing over the quinoa, and fluff up with a fork. Transfer to a shallow dish and let cool.

3 Plunge the snow peas into a saucepan of boiling water for 30 seconds, then drain. Let dry, then slice each snow pea diagonally in two.

4 Carefully stir the snow peas, grapes, almonds, and chives into the quinoa.

5 Arrange the lettuce leaves around the edges of two plates. Pile the quinoa mixture in the center, drizzle with a little more sesame oil, and serve.

50

MELON

Juicy melon flesh is rich in vitamin C and a great source of potassium and carotenes, providing a wealth of health benefits.

We love melon as a refreshing, aromatic fruit—with a greater than 90 percent water content, it helps keep us hydrated and the juice needs no added sugar to make it palatable. Melon flesh varies in color from creamy to yellow to orange and red; in general, the deeper the color, the more carotenes (which protect against cancer and help heart health) the fruit contains. So cantaloupe and watermelon are two good varieties to choose. All melons are a great source of vitamin C for a healthy immune system and heart, and potassium, which helps prevent fluid retention and is vital for a healthy blood pressure level. Several varieties are high in bioflavonoids, plant chemicals that have anticancer, antiheart disease, and antiaging properties.

- An average slice of melon contains half a day's RDA of vitamin C for adults.
- High potassium content helps prevent fluid retention and high blood pressure.
- Soluble fiber content helps lower LDL blood cholesterol.
- Watermelon contains citrulline, an amino acid that improves blood flow to muscles, which can help during exercise.

Practical tips:
Try to buy melon still in its skin—if you choose prepared melon, its vitamin C content will be diminished. Wash and dry melons thoroughly before cutting to reduce the risk of food poisoning from dirty skin, and store all cut melon in the refrigerator. Try melon slices draped with Italian cured ham for a simple appetizer.

DID YOU KNOW?

In some parts of the world, roasted melon seeds are a popular snack—the seeds are a good source of magnesium, iron, zinc, and phosphorous.

NUTRIENTS PER AVERAGE SLICE CANTALOUPE (3½ oz EDIBLE PORTION)

Calories	34
Protein	0.8 g
Fat	Trace
Carbohydrate	8 g
Fiber	0.9 g
Vitamin C	37 mg
Potassium	267 mg
Beta-carotene	2,020 mcg

Melon, prosciutto ham, and pecorino salad

SERVES 4 (P) (N)

⅕ a watermelon (about
*   2 pounds), peeled,*
*   seeded, and thinly sliced*
⅔ a honeydew melon (about
*   2 pounds), peeled, seeded,*
*   and thinly sliced*
1 large cantaloupe (about
*   2 pounds), peeled, seeded,*
*   and thinly sliced*
5 ounces sliced prosciutto ham
1 ounce pecorino cheese,
*   finely shaved*
1 cup fresh basil

Dressing
¼ cup light olive oil
¼ cup aged sherry vinegar
salt and pepper, to taste

Method

1 Arrange the watermelon, honeydew melon, and cantaloupe slices
   on a large serving plate. Tear any large prosciutto ham slices in half,
   then fold them all over and around the melon.
2 To make the dressing, put the olive oil and sherry vinegar in a clean
   screw-top jar, season well with salt and pepper, screw on the lid,
   and shake well. Drizzle the dressing over the melon and ham.
3 Sprinkle with the pecorino and basil. Serve immediately.

51

FIGS

Both fresh and dried figs are a valuable source of dietary fiber and contain useful amounts of minerals for heart health.

Figs contain good amounts of dietary fiber, much of which is soluble, to help protect against heart disease. They also contain enzymes that have a mildly laxative effect, so they are helpful to aid a regular bowel. Figs are a good source of potassium, which regulates blood pressure, and they contain calcium, magnesium, and natural sterols, all of which are good for the heart. Calcium and magnesium also work together to keep bones healthy. Figs provide some iron, a mineral that can easily be in short supply on a gluten-free diet, and they contain antioxidant carotenes for eye health and to help lower the risk of some cancers.

- Contain several nutrients to promote heart health and reduce blood pressure.
- Fiber and enzymes help maintain good bowel movement.
- Minerals for bone health.
- Carotenes for healthy eyes.

Practical tips:
Fresh figs are best eaten raw, poached, or lightly broiled. They make a light appetizer or canapé—try stuffing them with soft mozzarella or ricotta cheese. They're ideal as a dessert or at breakfast. Try them with Greek yogurt and honey. Dried figs are also good this way or can be poached in water or juice to reconstitute. Dried figs have a similar nutrient profile to fresh, per fig.

DID YOU KNOW?

Blend dried figs with a little water to replace sugar in baking—they add a succulent and moist texture.

NUTRIENTS PER MEDIUM FRESH FIG

Calories	40
Protein	0.4 g
Fat	Trace
Carbohydrate	10.4 g
Fiber	1.6 g
Calcium	19 mg
Magnesium	9 mg
Potassium	125 mg
Beta-carotene	51 mcg

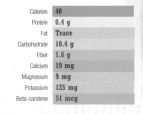

Tapioca figs

SERVES 6 (**C**) (**D**)

1 1/3 cups small tapioca pearls
2 cups rice milk
1/3 cup sugar
seeds from 2 cardamom pods,
    lightly crushed
1 bay leaf
1 tablespoon sunflower spread,
    plus extra for greasing
1/2 teaspoon orange flower water
6 fresh figs
pomegranate syrup, for drizzling

Method

1 Grease a 7-inch square cake pan. Put the tapioca and rice milk into a saucepan and bring to a boil. Reduce the heat and stir in the sugar, cardamom, bay leaf, and the spread.

2 Cover and cook gently, stirring often, for 20–25 minutes, until the grains are tender.

3 Remove and discard the bay leaf and cardamom pods, stir in the orange flower water, then spread into the pan and let cool. Chill in the refrigerator until set.

4 To serve, turn out the tapioca and cut into diamond shapes. Quarter the figs and arrange on plates with the tapioca shapes. Drizzle with pomegranate syrup and serve.

52 STRAWBERRIES

Strawberries are the fourth richest fruits in antioxidant compounds and have numerous health benefits. Full of soluble fiber, they're an excellent fruit to include in a gluten-free diet.

Strawberries, native to North America and Europe, are extremely rich in the antioxidant vitamin C—an average ⅔-cup/3½-ounce serving contains nearly a whole day's recommended daily amount for an adult. This essential vitamin helps boost the immune system, prevents arterial damage, speeds wound healing, aids iron absorption, and strengthens blood vessel walls. Strawberries also contain other antioxidants, such as anthocyanins and ellagic acid, which can block cancer cells and help prevent some cancers. And strawberries contain good amounts of dietary fiber, with a high proportion of artery- and digestive tract-friendly soluble fiber, folate, and potassium.

- Excellent source of vitamin C.
- Contains ellagic acid, a compound with anticancer and antioxidant properties.
- Contains anthocyanins, which can help lower LDL blood cholesterol.
- Useful source of fiber, potassium, folate, and zeaxanthin.

Practical tips:
Smaller strawberries tend to have higher levels of ellagic acid, which is concentrated in the red outer layer, and more flavor. Choose fruit that look plump and glossy—a dull appearance means they are past their best with less vitamin C. Only slice, if necessary, at the last minute, because cutting destroys the vitamin C.

DID YOU KNOW?

Wild strawberries—the ancestors of today's cultivated strawberries—grow easily in most yards and are an even richer source of nutrients than their giant modern counterparts.

NUTRIENTS PER AVERAGE SERVING
(⅔ cup/3½ oz)

Calories	32
Protein	0.7 g
Fat	0.3 g
Carbohydrate	7.7 g
Fiber	2 g
Folate	24 mcg
Vitamin C	59 mg
Potassium	153 mg
Zeaxanthin	26 mcg

Strawberry roll

SERVES 6 (v)

sunflower oil, for greasing
3 extra-large eggs
⅔ cup granulated sugar,
   plus extra to sprinkle
½ teaspoon almond extract
⅓ cup cornstarch
¾ cup ground almonds
   (almond meal)

Filling

1 cup cream cheese
1 tablespoon confectioners'
   sugar, plus extra for dusting
1½ cups hulled and sliced
   strawberries

Method

1 Preheat the oven to 350°F. Grease an 8 x 12-inch jellyroll pan and line it with parchment paper.

2 Put the eggs, sugar, and almond extract into a large bowl over a saucepan of hot, not boiling, water and whisk for about 10 minutes, until thick enough to hold a trail when the whisk is lifted. Remove from the heat and whisk in the cornstarch, then fold in the ground almonds.

3 Spread the batter into the prepared pan and bake in the preheated oven for 12–15 minutes, until just firm and lightly browned.

4 Place a sheet of parchment paper on the work surface and sprinkle with granulated sugar. Invert the pan over the paper to turn out the cake. Remove the lining paper and trim the edges from the cake. Cover with a clean dish towel and let cool.

5 To make the filling, beat together the cream cheese and confectioners' sugar, then spread it over the cake. Top with the sliced strawberries and carefully roll up the cake from one short edge.

6 Place on a serving plate with the seam underneath, and dust with confectioners' sugar to serve.

53

BLUEBERRIES

These popular berries are higher than most other fruits or vegetables in antioxidants, and they pack a powerful punch with many health benefits.

Because blueberries are so rich in nutrients, a relatively small amount (a ⅓-cup/1¾-ounce serving) can offer a good level of protection from various health problems. They contain at least 15 of the most-researched antioxidants. For example, they contain the compound pterostilbene, which is thought to be as effective as commercial medicines in lowering cholesterol, as well as helping to prevent diabetes and some cancers. They're high in anthocyanins, which can protect against heart disease and memory loss, and in anti-inflammatory, anticancer kaempferol. They are also a good source of vitamin C and dietary fiber, and they appear to help protect against urinary tract and digestive infections.

- Antioxidant and plant compound-rich berries.
- Contain cholesterol-lowering compound pterostilbene.
- Can help prevent many of the major diseases, including heart disease, diabetes, and cancers.
- Help beat urinary tract infections.

Practical tips:
The berries are delicious eaten raw (which helps to preserve their vitamin C content) but can also be lightly cooked in a small amount of water (the resulting juice is tasty and vitamin rich, too). They freeze well and lose almost none of their nutrients. Cook from frozen for best results. Add blueberries to your breakfast cereal or blend with yogurt for a smoothie. They will also boost the nutrient content of muffins, cakes, crisps, pies, and fruit salads.

NUTRIENTS PER AVERAGE SERVING
(⅓ CUP/1¾ OZ)

Calories	29
Protein	0.4 g
Fat	Trace
Carbohydrate	7.2 g
Fiber	1.2 g
Folate	34 mcg
Vitamin C	5 mg
Vitamin E	0.3 mg
Iron	0.7 mg
Potassium	39 mg
Lutein/Zeaxanthin	40 mcg

Yogurt with blueberries, honey, and nuts

SERVES 4 (**D**) (**N**)

3 tablespoons honey
¾ cup mixed unsalted nuts
½ cup Greek yogurt
1½ cups fresh blueberries

Method

1 Heat the honey in a small saucepan over medium heat. Add the nuts and stir until they are well coated. Remove from the heat and let cool slightly.

2 Divide the yogurt among four serving bowls, then spoon the nut mixture and blueberries over it and serve immediately.

54 CRANBERRIES

For several years, cranberries have been acknowledged for their role in helping us to good health and not without cause— they really are good for you.

DID YOU KNOW?

People taking warfarin should avoid eating cranberries or drinking cranberry juice because the berry interacts with the drug and can be dangerous.

NUTRIENTS PER 1 CUP/3½ OZ FRESH CRANBERRIES

Calories	46
Protein	0.4 g
Fat	Trace
Carbohydrate	12.2 g
Fiber	4.6 g
Vitamin C	13 mg
Vitamin E	1.2 mg
Carotenes	127 mcg

PER ⅓ CUP/1¾ OZ DRIED CRANBERRIES

Calories	154
Protein	Trace
Fat	0.7 g
Carbohydrate	41 g
Fiber	2.9 g
Vitamin C	Trace
Vitamin E	0.5 mg
Carotenes	17 mcg

Fresh cranberries are sour, so they are rarely eaten raw; but much of their goodness is preserved even when they are cooked. They are also popular when dried and sweetened. One of their biggest plusses is that they can help to prevent, or shorten the duration of, urinary tract infections, such as cystitis, and kidney and bladder stones. This is partly because they contain quinic acid and tannins, which have antibacterial properties. The high levels of these plant compounds may also help protect against stomach ulcers and heart disease and may have a beneficial effect on your digestive health, which may be helpful for people diagnosed with celiac disease. They are also a good source of the antioxidants vitamin C, vitamin E, and beta-carotene, and of soluble fiber, all of which can protect the heart and may lower the risk of some cancers.

- Help prevent and alleviate urinary tract infections.
- High soluble fiber content may help reduce HDL cholesterol.
- Help prevent digestive disorders and stomach ulcers.
- May protect against heart disease and cancer.

Practical tips:
Cranberries have been popular for decades as the major ingredient in cranberry sauce to go with turkey and game, but they are also excellent in jellies, preserves, and chutneys. Dried cranberries (usually with added sugar) are great in fruit salads, sprinkled on breakfast cereal, or added to muffins and other baked goods.

Chocolate, cranberry, and nut muffins

MAKES 12

2 cups quinoa flour

2 tablespoons unsweetened
    gluten-free cocoa powder

2 teaspoons gluten-free
    baking powder

¾ teaspoon gluten-free
    baking soda

½ teaspoon salt

1 stick unsalted butter,
    at room temperature

⅔ cup sugar

2 eggs, lightly beaten

1 teaspoon vanilla extract

finely grated zest of
    1 large orange

1 cup milk

¾ cup dried cranberries

⅓ cup coarsely chopped
    macadamia nuts

Method

1 Preheat the oven to 400°F. Place 12 muffin cups in the sections of
   a muffin pan.

2 Sift together the flour, cocoa powder, baking powder, baking soda,
   and salt into a bowl. Tip any bran remaining in the sifter into the
   bowl, mixing lightly with your fingers.

3 In a separate large bowl, beat together the butter and sugar for
   about 4 minutes, or until light and fluffy. Gradually beat in the eggs,
   vanilla extract, and orange zest. Beat in the milk and add the flour
   mixture, a little at a time, beating well after each addition. Fold in the
   cranberries and nuts.

4 Divide the batter equally among the muffin cups. Bake in the
   preheated oven for 15–20 minutes, until well risen and a toothpick
   inserted into the center comes out clean.

5 Transfer the muffins to a wire rack and let cool completely.

55

AVOCADO

The delicious avocado is packed with health-giving nutrients, which can be lacking on a gluten-free diet, and is one of the few fruits with an excellent and healthy fat content.

Avocado flesh is high in monounsaturated fat (which can help reduce LDL cholesterol and raise HDL cholesterol) and is high in beta-sterols, which also lower LDL. The fat has a high content of oleic acid, a fatty acid, and glutathione, both of which can lower the risk of some cancers. Avocados are also rich in antioxidant, immune system-boosting vitamin E, and potassium to help control blood pressure. And they are a good source of the minerals zinc and magnesium, a useful source of iron, and an excellent source of vitamin C. Intake of all these important nutrients can be low on a gluten-free diet.

- High monounsaturated fat and sterol content to help lower cholesterol.
- Oleic acid helps lower risk of cancer.
- Great source of minerals and vitamin C.
- High in vitamin E which helps protect the heart and boost the immune system.

Practical tips:

Avocados are best served completely ripe and raw, because cooking destroys some of the nutrients. The flesh discolors within minutes once cut, so brush cut surfaces with lemon juice or vinegar. Try with mixed salad greens and a classic vinaigrette dressing. You can use mild, nutty-flavor avocado oil in dressings or for cooking, because it has a high smoke point.

DID YOU KNOW?

If you want to speed up the ripening of an avocado, put it in a paper bag with a banana or an apple. The paper bag will trap the ethylene gas—a powerful ripening tool—produced by the fruits.

NUTRIENTS PER MEDIUM AVOCADO

Calories	227
Protein	2.6 g
Fat	21 g
Carbohydrate	12 g
Fiber	9.2 g
Vitamin B$_6$	0.39 mg
Vitamin C	12 mg
Vitamin E	3 mg
Iron	0.8 mg
Potassium	690 mg
Zinc	0.9 mg

Avocado and corn salad

SERVES 4 Ⓕ Ⓥ Ⓓ Ⓝ

1⅓ cups frozen corn kernels

1 large avocado, halved, pitted,
    peeled, and cut into cubes

12 cherry tomatoes,
    cut into quarters

½ red onion, finely chopped

1 small green bell pepper,
    halved, seeded, and cut
    into small chunks

⅔ cup shredded kale

⅔ cup coarsely chopped
    fresh cilantro

Dressing

finely grated zest and juice
    of 1 lime

2 tablespoons olive oil

salt and pepper, to taste

Method

1 Put the corn kernels into a saucepan of boiling water. Bring back to
   a boil, then simmer for 3 minutes. Drain into a colander, rinse with
   cold water, drain again, then transfer to a salad bowl.

2 To make the dressing, put the lime zest and juice and oil in a clean
   screw-top jar, season with salt and pepper, screw on the lid, and
   shake well to combine.

3 Add the avocado, tomatoes, onion, green bell pepper, kale, and
   cilantro to the salad bowl. Drizzle with the dressing and toss
   together. Spoon into four bowls and serve immediately.

56 APRICOTS

Apricots, both fresh and dried—packed with nutrients, rich in carbs, and low on the Glycemic Index—are an excellent addition to a gluten-free diet.

Fresh apricots contain a wide range of nutrients for health protection. Particularly important are vitamins A (in the form of beta-carotene) and E, both of which can be short on a gluten-free program. Other useful nutrients include vitamin C, folate, and potassium. Apricots are also ideal fruits for weight maintenance because they are a good source of fiber, are fat-free, and are low-GI. The semidried fruit is a good source of potassium, iron, and fiber, but the drying process loses vitamin C. Dried apricots are relatively high in calories, because their water content is diminished, so they are ideal as a snack when you're hungry, and their low-GI content will keep you full for a long time.

- Contain a range of carotenes, including cryptoxanthin, which may help to maintain bone health.
- High in total fiber and soluble fiber for heart protection and lowering cholesterol.
- Excellent source of potassium.
- A source of vitamin E for healthy skin and boosting the immune system.

Practical tips:
Apricots need to be fully ripe to maximize their carotene content. Cooking fresh apricots helps the body absorb the carotene and soluble fiber, and they are excellent in fruit crisps or poached in white wine. Dried apricots are good in couscous and other salads, chopped and added to cereal or a coleslaw, and stewed to serve with yogurt.

DID YOU KNOW?

Try to avoid dried apricot containing sulfites; these may trigger some allergies.

NUTRIENTS PER TWO MEDIUM FRESH APRICOTS (3½ oz)

Calories	31
Protein	0.9 g
Fat	Trace
Carbohydrate	7.2 g
Fiber	1.7 g
Vitamin C	6 mg
Vitamin E	0.6 mg
Iron	0.5 mg
Potassium	270 mg
Beta-carotene	766 mcg

PER 3 WHOLE SEMIDRIED APRICOT PIECES (1 oz)

Calories	47
Protein	1.2 g
Fat	Trace
Carbohydrate	10.8 g
Fiber	1.9 g
Vitamin C	Trace
Vitamin E	1.3 mg
Iron	1 mg
Potassium	414 mg
Beta-carotene	163 mcg

Millet porridge with apricot puree

SERVES 4   ⓒ Ⓕ Ⓥ Ⓓ Ⓟ Ⓝ

2 cups millet flakes
4 cups soy milk
pinch of salt
freshly grated nutmeg, to serve

Apricot puree
1 cup coarsely chopped
    dried apricots
1¼ cups water

Method

1 To make the apricot puree, put the apricots into a saucepan and cover with the water. Bring to a boil, then reduce the heat and simmer, half covered, for 20 minutes, until the apricots are tender. Use a handheld immersion blender, or transfer the apricots and any water left in the pan to a food processor or blender, and process until smooth. Set aside.

2 For the porridge, put the millet flakes into a saucepan and add the milk and salt. Bring to a boil, reduce the heat, and simmer, stirring often, for 15 minutes, or according to package directions, until cooked.

3 To serve, spoon into four bowls and top with the apricot puree and a little nutmeg.

57 MANGO

Mangoes are a rich source of several important nutrients and are one of the stars of the fruit bowl. They are particularly high in dietary fiber, crucial for a healthy digestive system.

The deep orange flesh of the mango is a clue to one of its major components—the potent antioxidant beta-carotene. This important health compound can protect against some cancers and heart disease. Mango also contains lycopene, a special type of carotene known to protect against prostate cancer, and polyphenols, linked with regulation of blood sugar levels. The fruit is also high in vitamin C—one fruit contains a whole day's RDA. Unlike many other fruits, they also contain a significant amount of the antioxidant vitamin E, which can boost the body's immune system and maintain healthy skin. Mangoes have a great fiber content, too—two-thirds of which is soluble—and good levels of potassium.

- High beta-carotene content, associated with cancer and heart protection.
- High levels of pectin—a soluble fiber which helps reduce LDL blood cholesterol.
- Rich in potassium for regulating blood pressure.
- Valuable source of vitamin C and polyphenols.

Practical tips:
Eat mangoes when they are completely ripe and aromatic. They are delicious eaten raw, for maximum vitamin C content, while their carotenes are better absorbed if you eat them with fat. Try Greek yogurt and mango for breakfast or a mango and chicken salad with an olive oil dressing for lunch.

DID YOU KNOW?

Mangoes—first cultivated in India 5,000 years ago—have natural tenderizing properties, making them a perfect ingredient for meat marinades.

NUTRIENTS PER AVERAGE MANGO (7 oz)

Calories	120
Protein	1.6 mg
Fat	0.7 g
Carbohydrate	30 g
Fiber	3.2 g
Folate	22 mg
Vitamin C	73 mg
Vitamin E	1.8 mg
Calcium	86 mcg
Potassium	336 mg
Zinc	1,280 mcg
Lutein/Zeaxanthin	46 mcg
Beta-carotene	297 mg

Mango sorbet

SERVES 4–6 (C) (N)

2 large ripe mangoes
juice of 1 lemon
pinch of salt
²⁄₃ cup sugar
3 tablespoons water

Method

1 Using a sharp knife, thinly peel the mangoes, holding them over a bowl to catch the juices. Cut the flesh away from the pit in the center, and put the flesh into a food processor or blender, reserving some slices for decoration. Add the reserved mango juices, the lemon juice, and salt and process to form a smooth puree. Push the mango puree through a nylon strainer into the bowl.

2 Put the sugar and water into a heavy saucepan and heat gently, stirring, until the sugar has dissolved. Bring to a boil, without stirring, then remove from the heat and let cool slightly.

3 Pour the syrup into the mango puree and mix well. Let cool, then chill the mango syrup in the refrigerator for 2 hours, or until completely cold.

4 If using an ice cream maker, churn the mixture in the machine, following the manufacturer's directions. Alternatively, freeze the mixture in a freezer-proof container, uncovered, for 3–4 hours, or until mushy. Transfer the mixture into a bowl and stir with a fork to break down the ice crystals. Return to the freezer and freeze for an additional 3–4 hours, or until firm. Cover the container with a lid for storing.

5 To serve, scoop into individual serving dishes and decorate with the reserved mango slices.

58

NECTARINES

Nectarines are an excellent choice for a summer fruit because they are full of vitamins and minerals. They are also a richer source of potassium than their close relatives, peaches.

The bright red skin and deep orange flesh of a nectarine means it is high in the compound beta-carotene, the antioxidant that is so important for the immune system. Beta-carotene can also be converted to vitamin A in the body—a vitamin linked with healthy skin, protection from harmful UV rays, and growth. Just one nectarine provides around one-quarter of your daily vitamin A requirements. The fruit is also rich in two special carotenes—lutein and zeaxanthin—to support eye health and vision. Nectarines are also a good source of vitamin C, contain a good range of the B vitamins, and a useful amount of minerals. They are low GI so their carb content won't cause a spike in your blood sugar levels.

- Rich in vitamin C.
- Excellent source of vitamin A for healthy skin.
- High in carotenes for eye health and vision.
- Low-GI fruit to help prevent blood sugar fluctuations.

Practical tips:
Ripe nectarines bruise easily, so treat them gently. They are delicious on their own, but try them in a salad with blue cheese and crispy lettuce, or sprinkle them with a little brown sugar and roast. Process the flesh in a blender, mix with yogurt, and freeze for a healthy iced dessert or snack.

DID YOU KNOW?

Nectarines are a mutant version of a peach with almost identical genes—they aren't related to the plum, as is often thought.

NUTRIENTS PER MEDIUM NECTARINE

Calories	62
Protein	1.5 mg
Fat	0.5 g
Carbohydrate	15 g
Fiber	2.4 g
Vitamin B5	0.3 mg
Niacin	1.6 mg
Vitamin C	7.7 mg
Vitamin E	1.0 mg
Potassium	285 mg
Lutein/Zeaxanthin	185 mcg
Beta-carotene	213 mcg

Stuffed nectarines with yogurt

SERVES 4 Ⓕ Ⓥ

4 ripe but firm nectarines
1 cup blueberries
1 cup raspberries
⅔ cup freshly squeezed
   orange juice
1–2 teaspoons honey,
   or to taste
1 tablespoon brandy (optional)
¼ cup Greek yogurt
1 tablespoon finely grated
   orange zest

Method

1 Preheat the oven to 350°F. Cut the nectarines in half, remove the pits, then put them into a shallow ovenproof dish.

2 Mix the blueberries and raspberries together in a bowl and use to fill the hollows left by the nectarine pits. Spoon any extra berries around the edge.

3 Mix together the orange juice and honey, and brandy, if using, in a small bowl and pour the liquid over the fruit. Blend the yogurt with the orange zest in another bowl and let chill in the refrigerator until required.

4 Bake the berry-filled nectarines in the preheated oven for 10 minutes, or until the fruit is hot. Serve immediately with the orange-flavor yogurt.

59

PAPAYA

The tropical papaya fruit has a range of vital nutrients that can help keep your digestive system healthy and even prevent some cancers.

The fruit is unique in that it contains papain, an enzyme that helps digest proteins, and chymopapain, which is strongly linked with preventing colonic cancer, may help to calm inflammation in the digestive tract and may also help protect against other digestive problems. Papaya is rich in the carotene lycopene—it is believed that by eating it regularly, men can reduce their likelihood of getting prostate cancer. The high potassium and useful magnesium content means the fruit is ideal for helping to reduce high blood pressure. Half a fruit provides almost a day's recommended vitamin C intake and is also a useful source of calcium for healthy bones.

• Contains the enzyme papain to help the digestive system.
• Large lycopene content helps to prevent prostate cancer.
• Potassium and magnesium to reduce high blood pressure.
• Good source of vitamin C and calcium.

Practical tips:
A ripe papaya usually has orange and yellow, instead of green, skin. If using papaya in a fruit salad, add it just before serving, because the papain can oversoften other fruits in the bowl. The papain also prevents gelatin from setting, so papaya shouldn't be used in gelatins. Papaya juice is an excellent marinade to tenderize meat, or add it to a casserole.

DID YOU KNOW?

The Mayans used to worship papaya trees and called them the "Tree of Life." Papayas were said to be one of the favorite fruits of the explorer Christopher Columbus.

NUTRIENTS PER HALF LARGE PAPAYA (3½ oz EDIBLE PORTION)

Calories	43
Protein	0.5 mg
Fat	0.3 g
Carbohydrate	10.8 g
Fiber	1.7 g
Folate	37 mcg
Vitamin C	61 mg
Potassium	182 mg
Lutein/Zeaxanthin	89 mcg
Beta-carotene	274 mcg
Lycopene	1,828 mcg

Chicken, papaya, and avocado salad

SERVES 2   (V) (D) (P) (N)

2 boneless, skinless chicken
   breasts, about 5½ ounces
   each
2 tablespoons olive oil
4 cups peppery salad greens,
   such as arugula, mizuna,
   chicory, mâche, and
   watercress
1 large papaya, peeled, seeded,
   and thickly sliced
1 ripe avocado, peeled, pitted,
   and thickly sliced
¼ cup toasted hazelnuts, halved
2 tablespoons quinoa sprouts
   or alfalfa sprouts
salt and pepper, to taste

Dressing
2 tablespoons lime juice
⅓ cup hazelnut oil
salt and pepper, to taste

Method

1 Place the chicken breasts on a board. With the knife parallel to the board, slice each breast in half horizontally to make four cutlets.

2 Place the cutlets between two sheets of plastic wrap and pound with a rolling pin to a thickness of about ⅜ inch.

3 Heat the oil in a large skillet. Add the chicken and cook over medium–high heat for 3–4 minutes on each side, until golden on the outside and no longer pink in the middle. Transfer to a warm plate and season with salt and pepper.

4 Slice the chicken lengthwise into ¾-inch-wide strips.

5 Divide the salad greens between two plates. Arrange the chicken, papaya, and avocado on top. Sprinkle with the hazelnuts and quinoa sprouts.

6 To make the dressing, whisk together all the ingredients until smooth and creamy. Pour it over the salad and serve immediately.

60 PLUMS

Widely available in many varieties, plums are rich in special phenolic compounds—antioxidants that protect the brain as well as the heart—and compounds beneficial to colon health.

Plums have been much researched because of the health-giving phenolic compounds they contain. These (neochlorogenic and chlorogenic acid) are particularly good at neutralizing the free radicals made in our bodies that are believed to contribute to disease and the aging process. Another chemical in plums (hydroxycinnamic acid) is particularly beneficial for the colon and linked with lower risk of colon cancer. Red/purple varieties are also rich in anti-inflammatory anthocyanins and have higher antioxidant levels than yellow plums. Dried or semidried plums (or prunes) are a healthy dried fruit snack with concentrated antioxidant power and a high potassium and iron content.

- Rich in phenolic compounds with strong antioxidant action.
- Contain chemicals particularly beneficial for the colon.
- Low-GI rating—useful for weight-loss plans and diabetics.
- Good source of carotenes for protection from cancer and eye health.

Practical tips:
Plums contain their highest levels of antioxidants when completely ripe, so don't eat them underripe. Cooked plums (halved, pitted, and cooked in a little water) will contain almost as many nutrients as when raw—make sure you eat the juice, too. Freeze for use in pies, desserts, and breakfast compotes.

DID YOU KNOW?

Plums are native to China where they have been eaten, for more than 2,000 years. There are over 100 varieties in commercial cultivation.

NUTRIENTS PER MEDIUM PLUM

Calories	30
Protein	0.5 mg
Fat	Trace
Carbohydrate	7.5 g
Fiber	0.9 g
Vitamin C	6.3 mg
Potassium	104 mg
Lutein/Zeaxanthin	48 mcg
Beta-carotene	125 mcg

Plum pancakes

SERVES 6   Ⓓ

8 plums, pitted and cut into
    quarters
½ cup maple syrup
1 tablespoon lemon juice
1 star anise
1¾ cups gluten-free
    all-purpose flour
1½ teaspoons gluten-free
    baking powder
2 eggs, beaten
1 cup sweetened soy milk
½ cup plain yogurt
1 tablespoon sunflower oil,
    plus extra for greasing

Method

1 Put the plums, maple syrup, lemon juice, and star anise into a
saucepan and heat until almost boiling. Reduce the heat, cover,
and cook gently for 8–10 minutes, stirring occasionally, until tender.

2 Put the flour, baking powder, eggs, milk, yogurt, and oil in a blender
or food processor and blend to a smooth batter.

3 Lightly grease a large, heavy skillet and heat until hot. Drop
tablespoonfuls of the batter into the pan and cook for 5–6 minutes,
turning once, until golden and set. Cook, in batches, until all the
batter is used.

4 To serve, stack the pancakes on serving plates and spoon the
plums and juices over them.

5

Vegetables

Whatever flavor, nutrient, or color you want on your plate,
there is a vegetable for you. Some are high in starches and
so can help boost your carb intake, which is sometimes hard
to maintain on a gluten-free diet; most are rich in soluble
and insoluble fiber for a healthy digestive system; and all
come packed with a huge variety of disease-preventing plant
compounds. Folate, magnesium, potassium, and iron are
just some of the vitamins and minerals that vegetables have
in abundance to help you to optimum health.

(C) High in carbohydrate

(F) Good source of fiber

(V) Rich in vitamins and minerals

(D) Particularly good for digestive health

(P) High in protein

(N) Nutrient boost for gluten-free diet

61

BEETS

Beets are a valuable food for anyone who experiences digestive problems and intolerances. Food scientists have recently discovered just how rich they are in nutrients and compounds that can help boost our health in several ways.

Beet are rich in betaine—a compound that helps improve digestion and nutrient absorption, reduce bloating, calm food intolerances, and control yeast and bacterial growth. The nitrates in the root can also raise HDL cholesterol, protect against blood clots, and lower high blood pressure significantly for up to 24 hours. Beets are high in the soluble fiber pectin, which plays a role in removing toxins from the body and can boost the work of the liver. And studies suggest that beet juice may even help increase stamina during aerobic exercise and reduce fatigue.

• Contains betaine to help with several digestive problems.
• Contains nitrates for heart and arterial health.
• Can help increase stamina for exercise.
• A good source of iron, magnesium, and the B vitamins and vitamin C.

Practical tips:
When you cook beets, leave 2 inches of stalk and the long "tail." This will prevent the beet from "bleeding" and losing color and nutrients as it cooks. Boil whole until tender, or bake brushed with oil. Beets can also be eaten raw—peel and grate into winter salads or make a nutritious juice. Use the leaves as you would spinach.

DID YOU KNOW?

Beets have a high sugar content for a vegetable, but it is released slowly into the body instead of the sudden rush that results from eating cane sugar.

NUTRIENTS PER MEDIUM BEET
(3½ oz)

Calories	43
Protein	1.6 mg
Fat	Trace
Carbohydrate	9.6 g
Fiber	2.8 g
Folate	109 mcg
Vitamin C	5 mg
Iron	0.8 mg
Magnesium	23 mg
Potassium	325 mg

Spiced beet and cucumber tzatziki

SERVES 4 (F) (V) (D) (N)

2 cooked beets in natural juices,
    drained and diced
½ cucumber, diced
⅓ cup diced radishes
1 scallion, finely chopped
12 butterhead lettuce leaves

Dressing

⅔ cup Greek yogurt
¼ teaspoon ground cumin
½ teaspoon honey
2 tablespoons finely chopped
    fresh mint
salt and pepper, to taste

Method

1 To make the dressing, put the yogurt, cumin, and honey into
   a bowl, then stir in the mint and season with salt and pepper.

2 Add the beet, cucumber, radishes, and scallion, then toss
   gently together.

3 Arrange the lettuce leaves on a plate. Spoon a little of the salad
   into each leaf. Serve immediately.

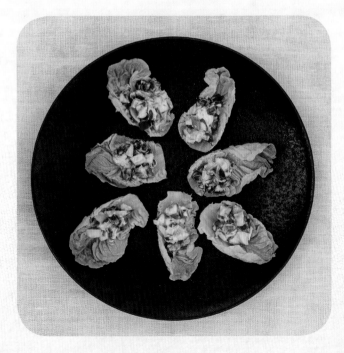

62

ONIONS

Onions are one of the best vegetables you can eat for your health—they can help combat cancer, heart disease, digestive problems, and inflammatory conditions, such as arthritis.

The pungent odor and flavor of onions indicates that they're rich in sulfides—compounds that boost immunity to disease, improve cell function, and help prevent several common cancers, including breast and ovarian cancer. One sulfur compound, onionin A, is unique to onions and has a particularly strong anti-inflammatory effect, which may help calm a sensitive digestive tract. Onions are particularly high in the polyphenol quercetin, which protects against cardiovascular disease, high cholesterol, and cancers (including colon cancer) and is powerfully inflammatory, helping minimize the symptoms of arthritis. Onions are also rich in a type of dietary fiber, called fructo-oligosaccharides, which help maintain a healthy balance of bacteria in the digestive tract, and in vitamin C.

- One of the best sources of polyphenols in the diet.
- Rich in sulfides to protect against cancer.
- Good source of dietary fiber to improve digestive tract health.
- Good source of vitamin C, calcium, potassium, and other minerals.

Practical tips:
The flavonoids in onion are mainly in the outer layers, so peel off as little as possible and try not to overbrown your onions when sautéing, because this destroys the beneficial compounds. Store onions in cool, dry, dark conditions to retain vitamin C.

DID YOU KNOW?

The substance that causes our eyes to stream when we peel an onion is propanethial S-oxide. It can be genetically removed from the vegetable, but that takes much of the beneficial sulfides with it, so commercial producers leave it in.

NUTRIENTS PER MEDIUM ONION (5½ OZ)

Calories	63
Protein	1.4 mg
Fat	Trace
Carbohydrate	15 g
Fiber	2.1 g
Folate	29 mcg
Vitamin C	9.6 mg
Calcium	33 mg
Magnesium	28 mg
Potassium	216 mg
Selenium	0.8 mcg

Potato and onion frittata

SERVES 4 (v) (N)

¼ cup olive oil

2 large onions, halved and
   thinly sliced

½ cup water

⅓ cup red quinoa, rinsed

6 red-skinned or white round
   potatoes (about 1½ pounds),
   peeled, halved lengthwise,
   and thinly sliced

9 eggs

½ teaspoon dried oregano

½ teaspoon salt

¼ teaspoon pepper

Method

1 Heat the oil in a skillet, add
  the onions, and gently sauté
  over low–medium heat for
  25 minutes, until golden
  and soft. Drain the onions,
  reserving the oil.

2 Meanwhile, put the water and
  quinoa into a small saucepan
  and bring to a boil. Cover
  and simmer over low heat for
  10 minutes, or until most of the
  liquid has been evaporated.

Remove from the heat, but
keep the pan covered for an
additional 10 minutes to let
the grains swell. Fluff up with
a fork.

3 While the quinoa is cooking,
  put the potatoes in a steamer
  and steam for 8 minutes, until
  just tender. Spread out to dry
  on a clean dish towel.

4 In a large bowl, beat the
  eggs with the oregano, salt,
  and pepper. Add the cooked
  onions, potatoes, and quinoa
  and stir to combine well.

5 Heat the reserved oil in a deep
  10-inch flameproof, nonstick
  skillet. Pour in the egg mixture,
  cover, and cook over low–
  medium heat for 15 minutes.
  Meanwhile, preheat the broiler.

6 Place the pan under the
  preheated broiler for 5 minutes
  to finish cooking the top of the
  frittata. Turn out onto a plate,
  cut into wedges, and serve
  immediately.

63 PARSNIPS

Low-cost parsnips are often overlooked in the kitchen, but they are nutritious and rich in carbohydrates, making them an ideal alternative to gluten-free grains.

Around 90 percent of a parsnip's calories are from carbohydrates, so they are a good alternative to potatoes or pasta. Parsnips come packed with potassium and folate, two nutrients important for cardiovascular health. Potassium helps protect you from high blood pressure, while folate helps lower your risk of heart disease and helps beat fatigue and weakness. Parsnips are also surprisingly high in vitamin C, supplying one-third of your RDA in a 5½-ounce portion, plus a fifth of your vitamin E needs. Both these antioxidant vitamins help prevent cell damage, which can lead to heart disease. The roots also contain useful levels of calcium, iron, magnesium, and zinc—four minerals often in short supply in a gluten-free diet.

- Starchy root vegetable with excellent levels of many vitamins and minerals.
- High potassium content for cardiovascular health.
- Rich in folate.
- High in the antioxidant vitamins C and E.
- Useful range of minerals ideal for a gluten-free diet.

Practical tips:
Highly versatile, parsnips can be roasted, boiled, or steamed; sliced into a gratin with cheese sauce; mashed or made into a soup; and even used instead of potatoes for homemade chips. Avoid really large roots that may be woody.

DID YOU KNOW?

Parsnips are related to carrots and are ideal to grow over winter, when frosts give the root a superior flavor. In Roman times, parsnips were thought to be an aphrodisiac.

NUTRIENTS PER MEDIUM PARSNIP
(5½ oz)

Calories	113
Protein	1.8 g
Fat	0.4 g
Carbohydrate	27 g
Fiber	7.4 g
Folate	101 mcg
Vitamin C	25 mg
Calcium	54 mg
Iron	0.9 mg
Magnesium	44 mg
Potassium	563 mg
Zinc	0.9 mg

Spiced parsnip gratin with ginger cream

SERVES 4 ⓕ ⓝ

butter, for greasing
3 large parsnips (about
 1½ pounds), thinly sliced
2 cups heavy cream
1 cup gluten-free
 vegetable stock
1 garlic clove, crushed
1-inch piece fresh ginger,
 coarsely chopped and
 crushed in a garlic press
¼ teaspoon white pepper
⅛ teaspoon freshly grated
 nutmeg, plus extra to garnish
sea salt
snipped fresh chives, to garnish

Method

1 Lightly grease a large gratin dish. Put the parsnips into a steamer set over a saucepan of boiling water. Steam for 3 minutes, until barely tender, shaking halfway through cooking. Transfer to the prepared dish and lightly season with salt.

2 Preheat the oven to 350°F. Gently heat the cream and stock in a saucepan with the garlic and ginger. Do not let the mixture boil. Add the pepper, nutmeg, and sea salt to taste.

3 Pour the hot cream mixture over the parsnips. Cover the dish with aluminum foil and bake in the preheated oven for 20 minutes, with an oven pan underneath to catch any drips.

4 Remove the foil and bake for an additional 15–20 minutes, until golden on top.

5 Sprinkle with a little more nutmeg and some chives and serve.

64 POTATOES

Potatoes are rich in starch and are ideal for boosting the carbohydrate intake of anyone following a gluten-free diet. They also come packed with essential vitamins and minerals.

Potatoes are a main source of vitamin C in our diets, containing nearly half of a day's RDA in an average 5½-ounce portion. In addition, they are a particularly good source of the complete range of B vitamins, which work together in our bodies for a healthy nervous system, food digestion, and metabolism. Their huge potassium content and their newly discovered content of compounds called kukoamines both work well to lower blood pressure. The tubers also contain useful levels of iron and magnesium. Potato flour is made from cooked, dehydrated, and ground potatoes—the flour loses much of the B and C vitamins in the drying process, but it can be a useful starchy flour mixed with others in gluten-free baking.

- A healthy gluten-free source of starchy carbohydrates.
- Rich in the B vitamins and vitamin C.
- Potassium and kukoamine content lowers blood pressure.
- Useful source of iron and magnesium.

Practical tips:
Potatoes will give you more fiber if you eat the skins, and potatoes cooked in their skin also have a much lower GI (and will keep you feeling fuller for longer) than peeled, mashed potatoes. Depending on the recipe, potato flour may be used as a substitute for wheat flour or as a thickener in casseroles.

DID YOU KNOW?

Potatoes are the most grown and most popular vegetable throughout the world and were first grown in the Andes in South America at least 7,000 years ago.

NUTRIENTS PER MEDIUM POTATO WITH SKIN (5½ oz)

Calories	104
Protein	2.4 g
Fat	Trace
Carbohydrate	24 g
Fiber	3.6 g
Vitamin B$_5$	0.4 mg
Vitamin B$_6$	0.3 mg
Folate	27 mcg
Niacin	1.6 mg
Vitamin C	30 mg
Iron	0.8 mg
Magnesium	32 mg
Potassium	611 mg

Spicy baked potatoes

SERVES 4   Ⓒ Ⓕ Ⓥ Ⓝ

4 large baking potatoes
1 tablespoon vegetable oil
  (optional)
1 (15½-ounce) can chickpeas,
  drained and rinsed
1 teaspoon ground coriander
1 teaspoon ground cumin
¼ cup chopped fresh cilantro
⅔ cup low-fat plain yogurt
salt and pepper, to taste
salad greens, to serve

Method

1 Preheat the oven to 400°F. Scrub the potatoes and pat them dry with absorbent paper towels. Prick the potatoes all over with a fork, brush with oil (if using), and season with salt and pepper. Put the potatoes onto a baking sheet and bake in the preheated oven for 1–1¼ hours, or until cooked through. Cool for 10 minutes.

2 Meanwhile, put the chickpeas into a large mixing bowl and mash with a fork or potato masher. Stir in the ground coriander, cumin, and half the chopped fresh cilantro. Cover the bowl with plastic wrap and set aside.

3 Halve the cooked potatoes and scoop the flesh into a bowl, keeping the shells intact. Mash the flesh until smooth and gently mix into the chickpea mixture with the yogurt. Season with salt and pepper. Place the potato shells on a baking sheet and fill with the potato and chickpea mixture. Return the filled potatoes to the oven and bake for 10–15 minutes, until heated through.

4 Garnish the potatoes with the remaining chopped cilantro and serve with salad greens.

65

RUTABAGA

Rutabaga is one of the lowest-calorie—
and cheapest—of all root vegetables,
but, nevertheless, it contains several
vital nutrients in good amounts.

The typical rutabaga has purple skin and a cream-color flesh that turns yellow when cooked. This yellow flesh is a good source of carotenes, good for heart health and protecting against cancer. Other important chemicals include glucosinolates, which can also help reduce the risk of getting cancer. Rutabaga contains a good level of vitamin C, with nearly half of your RDA in a 3½-ounce serving, about one-quarter of a root. Vitamin C is an immune-boosting and antioxidant vitamin that can help keep skin in good condition. There's also calcium here, for healthy bones and teeth, and potassium. Both these minerals help regulate blood pressure.

- Source of cancer-preventing and heart-protecting carotenes.
- Contains glucosinolates, which are also thought to prevent cancers.
- Good source of vitamin C for boosting the immune system.
- Provides calcium and potassium.

Practical tips:
Rutabaga is best either cubed and boiled until tender, then mashed with olive oil or canola oil, or sliced and roasted as you would roasted potatoes. The tasty flesh can also be finely chopped and used in a winter soup with kale and onions and is also good mashed half and half with carrot, parsnip, or potato, which makes a delicious topping for a casserole.

DID YOU KNOW?

When rutabaga was first cultivated, it was known as the turnip-rooted cabbage (it is a member of the brassica family). In 1780, Sweden introduced the vegetable into the UK, hence why it is now known as the "swede" in most of the UK.

NUTRIENTS PER ¼ RUTABAGA (3½ oz)

Calories	24
Protein	0.7 g
Fat	0.3 g
Carbohydrate	5 g
Fiber	1.9 g
Folate	31 mcg
Niacin	1.2 mg
Vitamin C	31 mg
Calcium	53 mg
Potassium	170 mg
Carotenes	350 mcg

Roasted root vegetables with garlic

SERVES 4   (c)(f)(v)(n)

1 small rutabaga
2 large carrots
2 parsnips
3 red-skinned or white
   round potatoes
1 large red onion, sliced
8 large garlic cloves, unpeeled
1 teaspoon ground cumin
1 teaspoon ground coriander
3 tablespoons olive oil or
   canola oil
½ cup gluten-free vegetable
   stock
1 tablespoon lemon juice
1½ teaspoons honey
salt and pepper, to taste

Method

1 Preheat the oven to 375°F. Peel all the vegetables. Cut the rutabaga, carrots, and parsnips into thick sticks and slice the potato into ¼-inch-thick circles.

2 Put all the vegetables into a large roasting pan. Add the garlic, spices, salt and pepper, and the oil and toss together until combined. Spread the vegetables out until they cover the bottom of the pan. Place in the preheated oven and roast for 25 minutes.

3 Remove the pan from the oven and turn all the vegetables over, using a spatula. Combine the stock, lemon juice, and honey and sprinkle over the vegetables, then return to the oven for 15 minutes, or until only a little liquid remains and the vegetables are golden and tender. Serve immediately.

66

SWEET POTATOES

Packed with nutrients, sweet potatoes are also rich in starches that can help regulate blood sugars, so they are an excellent food to include in a gluten-free diet.

Sweet potatoes are richer in nutrients than traditional potatoes and can be substituted for them in many recipes. They have a lower GI than potatoes and also, unusually, help boost blood levels of adiponectin, a hormone that helps regulate insulin in diabetics. They also contain plant sterols and pectin, both of which help lower LDL blood cholesterol. Sweet potatoes are also one of the best food sources of beta-carotene, which is antioxidant, anticancer, and helps boost the immune system. In addition, these supertubers are an excellent source of antioxidant vitamins and minerals, including vitamin E and magnesium, and the antioxidant protein sporamin.

• Rich content of carotenes with strong anticancer action.
• Sterols and pectin content helps reduce LDL cholesterol.
• Low GI and with ability to stabilize insulin, useful for diabetics.
• Antioxidant minerals and vitamin E to protect skin.

Practical tips:
Choose small to medium sweet potatoes with unmarked skins, because these will be more tender when cooked. Bake or roast as normal potatoes, or mash with a little oil (fat helps the body absorb carotene). Unlike potatoes, the skins are somewhat tough and chewy, so you should peel them off. Sweet potatoes are excellent in stews, soups, and casseroles.

DID YOU KNOW?

Sweet potatoes are often confused with yams, but the two are not related. White-fleshed yams, related to the lily, contain fewer nutrients and taste drier and less creamy than sweet potatoes, which are from the convolvulus family.

NUTRIENTS PER MEDIUM SWEET POTATO (5½ oz)

Calories	129
Protein	2.4 g
Fat	Trace
Carbohydrate	30.2 g
Fiber	4.5 g
Vitamin C	3.6 mg
Vitamin E	0.4 mg
Calcium	45 mg
Iron	0.9 mg
Magnesium	38 mg
Potassium	506 mg
Zinc	0.5 mg
Beta-carotene	12,760 mcg

Spicy sweet potato fries

SERVES 6   (C) (F) (D) (N)

*6 sweet potatoes (about
    2 pounds)*
*2 tablespoons vegetable oil,
    plus extra for greasing*
½ teaspoon salt
½ teaspoon ground cumin
¼ teaspoon cayenne pepper

Method

1 Preheat the oven to 450°F. Grease a large baking pan.
2 Peel the sweet potatoes and slice into ¼-inch-thick spears about
    3 inches long. Spread the sweet potatoes on the prepared baking
    tray and drizzle with the oil.
3 In a small bowl, combine the salt, cumin, and cayenne. Sprinkle
    the spice mixture evenly over the sweet potato spears and
    then toss to coat.
4 Spread the sweet potatoes out into a single layer and bake in the
    preheated oven for 15–20 minutes, or until cooked through and
    lightly browned. Serve immediately.

67 FAVA BEANS

Fava beans have an almost perfect balance of carbohydrate and protein and are ideal for boosting your gluten-free carbohydrate intake for the day.

Fava beans are an excellent vegetable source of protein and starch and so make a satisfying side dish or part of a main meal to boost your carb intake. These beans, however, have much more to recommend them. They are particularly high in dietary fiber and are exceptionally high in a form of soluble fiber called arabinose, which can help improve the blood lipid profile and reduce blood LDL cholesterol. They have a good level of vitamin C, with all its antioxidant benefits. Fava beans are also rich in a range of minerals from iron (which is vital to transport oxygen throughout our bodies) to magnesium and calcium (for healthy bones) and zinc (to boost the immune system).

- Good source of vegetable protein.
- Starchy vegetable helps boost carbohydrate intake.
- Rich in iron for healthy blood.
- A good source of calcium for bones.

Practical tips:
Fava beans are best eaten when young and tender—they retain most nutrients if the outer pale green shell of the individual beans is intact, but you can also slip it off and eat the bright green beans inside. They go well with fresh summer herbs, such as mint and parsley, and with lemon, bacon, and chicken. Alternatively, try them pureed with garlic to make a bean hummus.

NUTRIENTS PER ⅔ CUP/3½ OZ SHELLED FAVA BEANS

Calories	81
Protein	8 g
Fat	0.6 g
Carbohydrate	11.7 g
Fiber	6.5 g
Vitamin C	8 mg
Calcium	56 mg
Iron	1.6 mg
Magnesium	36 mg
Potassium	280 mg
Zinc	1 mg

Chilled fava bean soup

SERVES 6 (**F**)(**D**)(**P**)(**N**)

*3½ cups gluten-free
    vegetable stock*
*4⅓ cups shelled fresh young
    fava beans*
3 tablespoons lemon juice
*2 tablespoons chopped fresh
    summer savory*
salt and pepper, to taste
⅓ cup Greek yogurt, to serve
chopped fresh mint, to garnish

Method

1 Pour the stock into a large saucepan and bring to a boil. Reduce the heat to a simmer, add the fava beans, and cook for about 7 minutes, or until the beans are tender.

2 Remove the pan from the heat and let cool slightly. Transfer to a food processor or blender, in batches if necessary, and process until smooth. Push the mixture through a strainer set over a bowl.

3 Stir in the lemon juice and summer savory and season with salt and pepper. Let cool completely, then cover with plastic wrap and chill in the refrigerator for at least 3 hours.

4 To serve, ladle into chilled bowls or glasses, top each with a tablespoon of yogurt, and garnish with mint. Serve immediately.

68 PEAS

Either freshly picked or frozen, peas are a versatile and rich source of vitamin C and several other important nutrients and plant chemicals, including soluble fiber to help digestion.

Peas contain more protein than most vegetables and have a high fiber content, including the soluble fiber pectin to aid digestion and lower LDL blood cholesterol. They are particularly high in vitamin C, a heart-protective antioxidant, and in the B vitamins folate and niacin. They are also rich in the carotenoids lutein/zeaxanthin (for healthy eyes) and high in all the major minerals (calcium, iron, magnesium, and zinc), which can be lacking on a gluten-free diet. And these little nutrient stores are packed with several anti-inflammatory, anticancer, and antidiabetes chemicals, including pisumsaponins and pisomosides that are found almost exclusively in peas.

- Rich in fiber and soluble fiber for digestive and artery health.
- High in antioxidants, including vitamin C.
- Contain a great range of important minerals.
- Packed with disease-preventing phytochemicals.

Practical tips:
Buy peas in the pod young—as they age, the sugars turn to starch and give them a mealy texture and flavor. Young pods (snow peas or sugar snap peas) can be eaten with the immature peas inside. Eat young, small peas raw to glean the most vitamin C. To cook peas, steam lightly or boil in as little water as possible (vitamin C content leaches into water during cooking).

DID YOU KNOW?

Frozen peas can often contain more vitamin C and other nutrients than fresh peas, because they are frozen within hours of picking to retain nutrients. Store-bought peas in their pods may be several days old.

NUTRIENTS PER ⅔ CUP/3½ OZ SHELLED PEAS

Calories	81
Protein	5.4 g
Fat	0.4 g
Carbohydrate	14.5 g
Fiber	5.1 g
Folate	65 mcg
Niacin	2.1 mg
Vitamin C	40 mg
Calcium	25 mg
Iron	1.5 mg
Magnesium	33 mg
Potassium	244 mg
Zinc	1.2 mg
Lutein/Zeaxanthin	2,477 mcg
Beta-carotene	450 mcg

Peas with lettuce

SERVES 4–6   (F) (V)

2 tablespoons butter, plus an
  extra pat
1 teaspoon sunflower oil
1 ounce chopped bacon
1 shallot, finely chopped
2 cups shelled peas
1¼ cups gluten-free vegetable
  stock or water
1 small butterhead lettuce,
  cored and shredded
2 tablespoons chopped
  fresh chervil
salt and pepper, to taste

Method

1 Melt the butter with the oil in a large saucepan over medium heat.
   Add the bacon and stir for 3 minutes. Add the shallot and continue
   cooking for an additional 3 minutes.

2 Add the peas and stock and season with salt and pepper (but
   remember that the bacon is salty). Cover the pan and bring to
   a boil over high heat, then uncover, reduce the heat slightly, and
   simmer for 5 minutes.

3 Add the lettuce and continue to simmer, uncovered, until the peas
   are tender and the liquid has evaporated. Stir in a pat of butter, then
   taste and adjust the seasoning, if necessary. Stir in the chervil and
   serve immediately.

69

TOMATOES

Tasty tomatoes have plenty to offer nutritionally and can help protect us from cardiovascular disease and cancer.

Tomatoes are packed with carotenes, particularly lycopene, which is strongly linked with protection from prostate cancer (one of the most common cancers in men), and boosting heart health. Tomatoes are also rich in salicylates, which have an antiblood-clotting effect. Several other antioxidants, including vitamin C, quercetin, and lutein, are found in tomatoes in good amounts. They are low in calories but high in potassium, which helps to regulate blood pressure and body fluids, and they contain useful amounts of dietary fiber. Kaempferol and antibacterial glycosides found in tomatoes may help lessen digestive tract sensitivity.

- Excellent source of lycopene to protect against prostate cancer.
- Rich in potassium to help regulate blood pressure and prevent fluid retention.
- Great source of antioxidants, such as quercetin, lutein, and vitamin C.
- Contain salicylates, which have an antiblood-clotting effect.

Practical tips:
Tomatoes ripened on the vine contain more lycopene than those ripened after picking, and it is better absorbed when eaten with some oil as a salad dressing or with olive oil for cooking. Lycopene is also more active in processed tomato products, such as ketchup, tomato paste, and tomato juice, than it is in raw tomatoes. The skin contains more antioxidants than the flesh, while the seeds are high in salicylates. Remove raw tomatoes from the refrigerator an hour before serving for the best flavor.

DID YOU KNOW?

Often thought of as a vegetable but actually a fruit, tomatoes are one of our most popular foods and come from the same nightshade family as potatoes and eggplants.

NUTRIENTS PER TOMATO (3½ oz)

Calories	18
Protein	0.9 g
Fat	0.2 g
Carbohydrate	3.9 g
Fiber	1.2 g
Vitamin C	13.7 mg
Vitamin E	0.5 mg
Potassium	237 mg
Lutein/Zeaxanthin	123 mcg
Lycopene	2,537 mcg

Meatballs with tomato sauce

SERVES 4 (V)(P)(N)

1 (28-ounce) can diced tomatoes
5 garlic cloves, crushed
2 teaspoons dried oregano
⅔ cup olive oil
½ teaspoon salt
chopped fresh flat-leaf parsley
    and freshly grated Parmesan
    cheese, to serve

Meatballs

1 small onion, grated
finely grated zest of 1 large
    lemon
2 garlic cloves, crushed
2 teaspoons dried oregano
1 teaspoon salt
¾ teaspoon pepper
1 extra-large egg white,
    lightly beaten
1 pound fresh ground pork
8 ounces fresh ground beef
¼ cup milled chia seeds

Method

1 First, make the meatballs. In a small bowl, mix together the onion, lemon zest, garlic, and oregano with the salt, pepper, and egg white.

2 Combine the pork and beef in a large bowl. Add the egg white mixture and use a fork to mix together well. Mix in the chia seeds and let stand.

3 Meanwhile, put the tomatoes into a large saucepan with the garlic and oregano, ¼ cup of the oil and the salt. Bring to a boil, then simmer briskly, uncovered, for 30 minutes, until thickened.

4 Divide the meat mixture into 20 balls, rolling them in the palm of your hand until firm.

5 Heat the remaining oil in a large skillet. Add the meatballs and cook for about 8 minutes, turning frequently, until brown all over. Transfer to paper towels to drain, then add to the tomato sauce and simmer for 5 minutes.

6 Transfer the meatballs and sauce to plates, sprinkle with parsley, and serve with Parmesan.

70 EGGPLANT

A glossy, purple eggplant is not only attractive but also contains a feast of different vitamins and minerals, as well as plant chemicals to boost brainpower.

Eggplants contain several antioxidant compounds, including one interesting flavonoid called nasunin. This helps to protect brain cells, particularly the fatty cells, from damage and may help boost brainpower and memory. The vegetable also contains terpenes, which can relax the blood vessels and may offer protection against high blood pressure and high cholesterol. The high potassium levels will help to boost that effect. One-third of the vegetable's extremely high fiber content is in the form of soluble fiber, which helps slow down the rate of food digestion and is helpful for anyone with a sensitive digestive tract. Eggplants also contain magnesium, calcium, vitamin C, folate, and vitamin E.

- Fiber content aids good digestion.
- Contains the flavonoid nasunin, which may boost brain function.
- Terpenes and potassium protect against heart and arterial disease.
- Good range of vitamins and minerals.

Practical tips:
Most commercially grown eggplants no longer have a slightly bitter taste, so it's not necessary to salt them before use. Cut eggplants turn brown quickly and spoil, so don't slice until you need to cook them. Eggplants soak up a lot of fat if fried, so broil or bake instead. Simply brush the pieces with oil beforehand.

DID YOU KNOW?

Eggplants were first cultivated in the Far East 2,500 years ago, but they were not widely used as a food until around 300 years ago due to the bitter taste of the original cultivars.

NUTRIENTS PER HALF MEDIUM EGGPLANT (8 oz)

Calories	55
Protein	2.3 g
Fat	0.4 g
Carbohydrate	13 g
Fiber	7.8 g
Folate	50 mcg
Vitamin C	5 mg
Vitamin E	0.7 mg
Calcium	21 mg
Magnesium	32 mg
Potassium	527 mg

Eggplant stew with polenta

SERVES 4   Ⓕ Ⓥ Ⓓ Ⓝ

1 eggplant, diced
3 tablespoons olive oil
1 large onion, thinly sliced
1 carrot, diced
2 garlic cloves, chopped
2 cups sliced mushrooms
2 teaspoons ground coriander
2 teaspoons cumin seeds
1 teaspoon chili powder
1 teaspoon ground turmeric
2½ cups canned diced tomatoes
1¼ cups gluten-free
    vegetable stock
½ cup chopped dried apricots
1 (15-ounce) can chickpeas,
    drained and rinsed
2 tablespoons chopped fresh
    cilantro, to garnish

Polenta
5 cups hot gluten-free
    vegetable stock
1½ cups quick-cook polenta
    or cornmeal

Method

1 Preheat the broiler to
medium. Toss the eggplant
in 1 tablespoon of the oil and
arrange in the broiler pan.
Cook under the preheated
broiler for 20 minutes, turning
occasionally, until softened and
beginning to blacken around
the edges—brush with more oil
if the slices become too dry.

2 Heat the remaining oil in
a large, heavy saucepan
over medium heat. Add the
onion and sauté, stirring

occasionally, for 8 minutes, or
until soft and golden. Add the
carrot, garlic, and mushrooms
and cook for 5 minutes. Add
the spices and cook, stirring
constantly, for another minute.

3 Add the tomatoes and stock,
stir, and bring to a boil. Reduce
the heat and simmer for
10 minutes, or until the sauce
begins to thicken and reduce.

4 Add the eggplant, apricots,
and chickpeas, partly cover,
and cook for 10 minutes,
stirring occasionally.

5 Meanwhile, to make polenta,
pour the hot stock into a large
saucepan and bring to a boil.
Pour in the polenta in a steady
stream, stirring constantly with
a wooden spoon. Reduce
the heat to low and cook for
1–2 minutes, or until thickened
to a mashed potato-like
consistency; alternatively,
prepare the cornmeal
according to package
directions. Serve the stew on
top of the polenta, sprinkled
with the fresh cilantro.

71

BELL PEPPERS

Colorful, sweet bell peppers contain high levels of carotenes for heart health and cancer protection, are full of vitamin C, and are a good source of folate, which are often low in a gluten-free diet.

Sweet peppers come in a variety of colors, but the purple, red, and orange bell peppers contain the highest levels of anticancer and heart protective carotenes and are one of the best vegetable sources of these chemicals. They are particularly rich in eye-protective lutein and zeaxanthin and in immune-boosting cryptoxanthin, an easily absorbed form of carotene. All colors of bell peppers are extremely rich in vitamin C, with a 3½-ounce serving providing nearly twice a day's recommended intake. They are also a good source of the B vitamin folate and a useful source of vitamin E, both of which can be lacking in a gluten-free diet.

- Contain several phytochemicals, which are strongly anticancer and boost the immune system.
- Good source of a range of vitamins and minerals.
- Extremely rich in antioxidant vitamin C.
- High lutein/zeaxanthin levels protect eyesight.

Practical tips:
Either cook bell peppers with some oil or use them raw in a salad dressed with oil, because the carotenes are better absorbed in our bodies when eaten with fat. Fresh bell peppers freeze well (slice and bag beforehand) for use in cooking and are also good blended into a vegetable smoothie.

DID YOU KNOW?

Bell peppers have recently been found to contain small amounts of nicotine, which researchers have found can help reduce the risk of Parkinson's disease without the drawbacks of smoking.

NUTRIENTS PER MEDIUM RED BELL PEPPER (3½ oz)

Calories	31
Protein	1 g
Fat	0.3 g
Carbohydrate	6 g
Fiber	2.1 g
Vitamin B$_6$	0.3 mg
Folate	46 mcg
Vitamin C	128 mg
Vitamin E	1.58 mg
Potassium	211 mg
Cryptoxanthin	735 mcg
Lutein/Zeaxanthin	77 mcg
Beta-carotene	2,436 mcg

Roasted pepper salad

SERVES 4 (V) (N)

2 red bell peppers, halved and
    seeded
2 yellow bell peppers, halved and
    seeded
1 red onion, coarsely chopped
2 garlic cloves, finely chopped
⅓ cup olive oil
4 ounces mini mozzarella
    cheese pearls, drained
2 tablespoons coarsely torn
    fresh basil
2 tablespoons balsamic vinegar
salt and pepper, to taste

Method

1 Preheat the oven to 375°F. Put the bell peppers, cut side up, in a
   shallow roasting pan. Sprinkle with the onion and garlic, season
   well with salt and pepper, and drizzle 3 tablespoons of the olive
   oil over them. Roast for 40 minutes, or until the bell peppers are
   tender. Let cool.

2 Arrange the cold bell peppers in a serving dish and pour over any
   juices left in the roasting pan. Sprinkle with the mozzarella and basil.

3 To make the dressing, whisk together the remaining olive oil and the
   balsamic vinegar, then drizzle it over the roasted peppers. Cover
   and marinate in the refrigerator for at least 2 hours before serving.

72

FENNEL

Fennel bulbs are high in nutrients that aid digestion, reduce inflammation, and can help to prevent some cancers. This is a particularly useful vegetable for anyone with a gluten intolerance.

Fennel contains a strong combination of plant chemicals, including the flavonoids rutin, quercetin, and kaempferol, all of which give it strong antioxidant activity. Its natural compounds are known to help calm the digestive system, helping to eliminate or ease flatulence, colic, and indigestion. One of the compounds in fennel, anethole, has also been shown to reduce inflammation and to help prevent the occurrence of cancer. It is also a good source of dietary fiber and calcium and contains a wide range of other nutrients, including vitamin C, folate, and iron. The high potassium content means that fennel is a diuretic, helping to eliminate surplus fluid from the body.

- Range of antioxidants for general health protection.
- Diuretic and digestive aid.
- Anti-inflammatory and anticancer.
- Good source of a range of vitamins and minerals.

Practical tips:
Florence (or Italian) fennel has a refreshing, slightly sweet, licorice flavor. All parts are edible—cut off the root end and peel away any tough outer skin. The stems are tough and stringy so use these to make soup. Fennel goes particularly well with chicken and fish—try baking small whole fish in aluminum foil on a bed of thinly sliced fennel. Roast or steam wedges of the bulb, or braise sautéed slices in vegetable stock. It is also delicious raw—thinly slice into salads.

DID YOU KNOW?

Florence fennel is related to parsley, carrots, dill, and cilantro. It is also closely related to the herb fennel, and the leafy tops of the bulb can be washed, chopped, and used as a garnish.

NUTRIENTS PER SMALL FENNEL BULB (3½ oz)

Calories	31
Protein	1.2 g
Fat	0.2 g
Carbohydrate	7.3 g
Fiber	3.1 g
Folate	27 mcg
Vitamin C	12 mg
Calcium	4.9 mg
Iron	0.7 mg
Potassium	414 mg

Quinoa salad with fennel and orange

SERVES 4 Ⓒ Ⓕ Ⓥ Ⓓ Ⓝ

4 cups gluten-free vegetable
  stock
1⅓ cups white quinoa, rinsed
  and drained
3 oranges
1 fennel bulb, thinly sliced, green
  feathery leaves reserved and
  torn into small pieces
2 scallions, finely chopped
¼ cup coarsely chopped
  fresh flat-leaf parsley

Dressing
juice of ½ lemon
3 tablespoons olive oil
pepper, to taste

Method

1 Bring the stock to a boil in a saucepan, add the quinoa, and simmer for 10–12 minutes, or until the germs separate from the seeds. Drain off the stock and discard, then spoon the quinoa into a salad bowl and let cool.

2 Grate the zest from two of the oranges and put it in a clean screw-top jar. Cut a slice off the top and bottom of each of the three oranges, then remove the peel in thin vertical slices and discard. Cut between the membranes to remove the orange segments, then squeeze the juice from the membranes into the jar.

3 Add the orange segments, fennel slices, scallions, and parsley to the quinoa in the salad bowl.

4 To make the dressing, add the lemon juice and oil to the jar, season with pepper, screw on the lid, and shake well. Drizzle the dressing over the salad and toss everything together. Garnish with the fennel leaves and serve immediately.

73

BUTTERNUT SQUASH

Butternut squash is one of the best sources of health-boosting carotenes. These powerful plant compounds help to keep skin in good condition and protect us from cancer and other diseases.

The orange-fleshed varieties of squash, including butternut, contain the highest levels of beneficial carotenes—one of these, beta-cryptoxanthin, is linked with protection from lung cancer. Squash is also one of the best sources of lutein and zeaxanthin, the carotenes associated with good eyesight, particularly in older age. Carotenes can also help reduce the inflammation associated with arthritis and arterial disease and lower the risk of colon and prostate cancers. Butternut squash is also a good source of antioxidant vitamins C and E. The essential minerals calcium, iron, and magnesium are all here in good amounts to keep bones strong and help keep fatigue at bay.

- Contains carotenes that are known to give us protection from many types of cancer.
- Rich in compounds that protect aging eyesight.
- Helps reduce inflammation and the symptoms of arthritis.
- Good source of antioxidant vitamins C and E.

Practical tips:
Squash has a smooth texture and nutty flavor ideal for both sweet and savory dishes. It goes particularly well with chicken and beef. Your body will absorb the carotenes better if you eat squash with a little oil, so roast cubes in olive oil or steam and dress with oil. Add roasted cubes to soups, vegetable chilis, and casseroles.

DID YOU KNOW?

Squash seeds are packed with nutrients. Wash them thoroughly and dry naturally or spread on a baking sheet, sprinkle with a little olive oil, and roast for 15 minutes at a low temperature for a nutritious snack.

NUTRIENTS PER 1 CUP/5½ OZ BUTTERNUT SQUASH

Calories	68
Protein	1.5 g
Fat	Trace
Carbohydrate	7.5 g
Fiber	3 g
Folate	41 mcg
Niacin	1.8 mg
Vitamin C	31 mg
Vitamin E	2.2 mg
Calcium	72 mg
Iron	1 mg
Magnesium	51 mg
Potassium	528 mg
Beta-carotene	6,339 mcg

Butternut squash stew

SERVES 4 (F) (V) (N)

1 tablespoon olive oil
1 onion, diced
3 garlic cloves, finely chopped
2 tablespoons tomato paste
2 teaspoons ground cumin
1 teaspoon ground cinnamon
1 teaspoon salt
¼ teaspoon cayenne pepper
½ butternut squash, peeled,
    seeded, and cut into
    bite-size pieces
½ cup brown lentils
2 cups gluten-free
    vegetable stock
1 tablespoon lemon juice

To garnish
¼ cup plain yogurt
2 tablespoons finely chopped
    fresh cilantro
2 tablespoons slivered almonds

Method

1 Heat the oil in a large saucepan over medium–high heat. Add the onion and garlic and cook, stirring occasionally, for about 5 minutes, or until soft.

2 Add the tomato paste, cumin, cinnamon, salt, and cayenne and give it a quick stir. Add the squash, lentils, and stock and bring to a boil. Reduce the heat to low and simmer, uncovered, stirring occasionally, for about 25 minutes, until the squash and lentils are tender.

3 Just before serving, stir in the lemon juice. Serve hot, garnished with a dollop of the yogurt and a sprinkling of cilantro and slivered almonds.

74 BROCCOLI

Broccoli contains a huge range of vitamins, minerals, and plant compounds that provide many health benefits, and it is a good source of fiber.

All types of broccoli—including baby broccoli varieties—are rich in phytonutrients, but the dark green and purple varieties have the highest levels. Broccoli contains sulforaphane, indoles, selenium, and immune-boosting vitamin C, all of which offer protection against breast cancer and other forms of cancer. The vegetable is also rich in carotenes, which help to lower LDL cholesterol, and protect against heart disease, and may also help improve memory and dry skin. Lutein and zeaxanthin found here protect eye health and vision, and broccoli is also one of the best vegetable sources of calcium to protect against osteoporosis.

- Contains sulforaphane and other nutrients for strong protection against cancer and heart disease.
- Carotenes protect against heart disease and may improve memory and skin.
- High calcium content helps build and protect bones.

Practical tips:
Three 1-cup/2⅓-ounce servings of broccoli a week will give you optimum protection against cancer. Lightly steam or stir-fry to get the most vitamin C and antioxidants from the vegetable, and don't forget the leaves and the stems—these are also edible and are full of fiber. Try instead of cauliflower for a tasty baked broccoli and cheese dish.

DID YOU KNOW?

Sulforaphane, found in broccoli, also appears to help protect against peptic ulcers by killing the bacteria that cause them.

NUTRIENTS PER 1½ CUPS/3½ OZ BROCCOLI

Calories	34
Protein	2.8 g
Fat	0.4 g
Carbohydrate	6.6 g
Fiber	2.6 g
Vitamin C	89 mg
Calcium	47 mg
Selenium	2.5 mcg
Lutein/Zeaxanthin	1,403 mcg
Beta-carotene	361 mcg

Buckwheat noodle and broccoli salad

SERVES 4 (**F**) (**V**) (**N**)

6 ounces gluten-free soba (buckwheat) noodles

1⅓ cups frozen edamame (soybeans)

3 cups small broccoli florets and thinly sliced stems

1 red bell pepper, halved, seeded, and thinly sliced

1 purple or orange bell pepper, halved, seeded, and thinly sliced

2 cups thinly sliced cremini mushrooms

2 cups sunflower sprouts or alfalfa sprouts

Dressing

2 tablespoons rice vinegar

2 tablespoons gluten-free tamari (Japanese soy sauce)

¼ cup rice bran oil

1½-inch piece of fresh ginger, peeled and finely grated

Method

1 Put cold water in the bottom of a steamer, bring to a boil, then add the noodles and frozen edamame beans and bring back to a boil. Put the broccoli in the top of the steamer, then put it on the steamer base, cover, and steam for 3–5 minutes, or until the noodles and vegetables are just tender. Drain and rinse the noodles and edamame, then drain again and transfer to a salad bowl. Add the broccoli, then let cool.

2 To make the dressing, put the vinegar, tamari, oil, and ginger into a clean screw-top jar, screw on the lid, and shake well. Drizzle the dressing over the salad and toss gently together.

3 Add the bell peppers and mushrooms to the salad and toss again. Spoon into four bowls, then top with the sprouts and serve immediately.

75 RED CABBAGE

This firm, purple-red cabbage is packed with a good range of phytochemicals for general health protection and many nutrients for digestive health.

Red cabbage is rich in compounds that protect us from disease. These include indoles, which have been linked to protection from breast, uterus, and ovarian cancers and can help protect against the signs of aging. It also contains sulforaphane, which can help block cancer-causing chemicals, and monoterpenes, which protect body cells from damage by free radicals. Red cabbage is much higher than other cabbages in carotenes, including lycopene, which offers protection from prostate cancer, and the glucosinolates, glutamine, and polyphenols found here appear to protect the lining of the intestines against attack from harmful bacteria and from ulcers. The purply leaves also contain anthocyanins, which may help prevent Alzheimer's disease. Additional benefits of eating red cabbage are the good levels of vitamin C and minerals, including calcium and selenium.

- Contains a variety of cancer-fighting compounds.
- Low in calories and ideal for weight-loss plans.
- Rich in the antioxidant vitamin C and several minerals.
- Anthocyanin content may protect against Alzheimer's disease.

Practical tips:
Red cabbage is an ideal ingredient for a coleslaw, with green cabbage and carrot. Alternatively, try it braised with chopped onion, apple, vinegar, and honey—delicious with roasted pork or lamb. Store wrapped in the refrigerator to retain its vitamin C content.

DID YOU KNOW?

The juice from red cabbage leaves can be used as a natural dye. It is also an antiseptic—useful to dab on any cuts that happen in the kitchen.

NUTRIENTS PER 1 CUP/3½ OZ RED CABBAGE

Calories	31
Protein	1.4 g
Fat	Trace
Carbohydrate	7.4 g
Fiber	2.1 g
Folate	18 mcg
Niacin	0.4 mg
Vitamin C	57 mg
Calcium	45 mg
Iron	0.8 mg
Potassium	243 mcg
Selenium	0.6 mcg
Lutein/Zeaxanthin	329 mcg
Beta-carotene	670 mcg

Red cabbage salad with eggplant dip

SERVES 4   (F) (V) (D) (N)

2 carrots
4 cups shredded red cabbage
1/3 cup raisins
4 cups mixed salad greens, such
    as a mixture of red-stemmed
    baby Swiss chard and mâche
juice of 1 orange
pepper, to taste

Dip

3 eggplants
3 garlic cloves, finely chopped
2 tablespoons tahini
3 tablespoons hemp oil
pepper, to taste

Method

1 To make the dip, preheat the broiler to high and remove the broiler
   rack. Prick both ends of each eggplant with a fork, put them in the
   broiler pan, and broil 2 inches away from the heat source, turning
   several times, for 15–20 minutes, until blackened. Let cool.

2 Shave the carrots into long, thin ribbons, using a swivel-blade
   vegetable peeler, then put them onto a serving plate. Add the
   cabbage, then sprinkle with the raisins and salad greens. Drizzle
   with the orange juice and season with a little pepper.

3 Cut the eggplants in half and scoop the soft flesh away from the
   blackened skins, using a tablespoon. Finely chop the flesh, then put
   it in a bowl. Add the garlic, tahini, and hemp oil, season with a little
   pepper, and mix together. Spoon into a serving bowl and nestle in
   the center of the salad to serve.

76

KALE

Curly kale is one of the best leafy greens to eat regularly—it contains the highest levels of antioxidants of all vegetables.

The dark green leaves contain various plant chemicals known for their antiaging properties and disease-fighting abilities. These include flavonoids, to lower LDL cholesterol, and indoles and isothiocyanates to protect against colon, bladder, breast, and prostate cancers. Kale is unusually rich in vitamins and minerals—a 1½-cup/3½-ounce portion contains almost twice the RDA of vitamin C, which helps the body absorb the vegetable's high iron content. A serving also gives around one-sixth of our daily calcium needs and is a good source of selenium, which helps fight cancer, and magnesium and vitamin E, which are important for heart health. The vitamin E and carotenes in kale also keep skin and eyes healthy. Kale also contains small amounts of anti-inflammatory omega-3 fats.

- Extremely high in vitamin C.
- Rich in flavonoids, indoles, and antioxidants to fight heart disease and cancers.
- Contains more calcium and iron than any other vegetable.
- Extremely rich in carotenes to protect eyes and help prevent cataracts.

Practical tips:
Store kale in a plastic bag in the refrigerator to prevent it from wilting. The outer, deepest green leaves contain the most carotenes and indoles. Steam or stir-fry, then let rest for a few minutes to maximize the potency of the antioxidants. Kale's strong, iron flavor marries well with beef, bacon, pasta, and potato, and it is delicious in vegetable soups.

DID YOU KNOW?

Kale is a great winter vegetable and becomes sweeter to eat once it has been through a winter frost.

NUTRIENTS PER 1½ CUPS/3½ OZ KALE

Calories	50
Protein	3.3 g
Fat	0.7 g
Carbohydrate	10 g
Fiber	2 g
Folate	29 mcg
Vitamin C	120 mg
Vitamin E	1.7 mg
Calcium	135 mg
Iron	1.7 mg
Magnesium	34 mg
Potassium	447 mg
Selenium	0.9 mcg
Lutein/Zeaxanthin	39,550 mcg
Beta-carotene	9,226 mcg

Kale and lima bean casserole

SERVES 6   Ⓕ Ⓥ Ⓓ Ⓝ

2 cups lima beans, soaked
   overnight
1 tablespoon cumin seeds
2 teaspoons dried oregano
3 tablespoons peanut oil
2 onions, chopped
2 garlic cloves, thinly sliced
1–3 fresh red or green chiles,
   seeded and sliced
1 (14½-ounce) can diced
   tomatoes
2 cups gluten-free vegetable
   stock
3 cups shredded kale
⅓ cup chopped fresh cilantro
juice of 1 lime
salt and pepper, to taste
2 avocados, cubed and tossed
   with lime juice, and red onion
   slivers, to garnish

Method

1 Drain the beans, put them into
a large saucepan, and cover
with water. Bring to a boil, boil
rapidly for 15 minutes, then
reduce the heat and simmer
for 30–45 minutes, until tender
but not disintegrating. Drain
and set aside.

2 Put the cumin seeds into a
small, dry skillet over medium
heat and fry until fragrant.
Add the oregano, cook
for a few seconds, then
immediately remove the
mixture from the pan.

3 Lightly crush the mixture in
a mortar with a pestle.

4 Heat the oil in a large,
flameproof casserole or Dutch
oven over medium heat. Add
the chopped onions and the
spice and herb mixture. Sauté
for 5 minutes, until the onions
are translucent. Add the garlic
and chiles and sauté for an
additional 2 minutes.

5 Stir in the tomatoes, beans,
and stock. Season with salt
and pepper and bring to a boil.
Reduce the heat, cover, and
simmer for 30 minutes, stirring
occasionally.

6 Increase the heat and stir in
the kale. Simmer, uncovered,
for 7 minutes, or until tender
but still brightly colored. Stir in
the cilantro and lime juice.

7 Ladle into soup plates,
garnish with the avocado
and red onion, and serve
immediately.

77 SPINACH

The strong iron taste of spinach gives a hint that this vegetable packs a punch in the nutrition department. New research also shows that it contains anti-inflammatory compounds that may help protect your digestive system.

NUTRIENTS PER 3½ CUPS/3½ OZ SPINACH

Calories	23
Protein	2.9 g
Fat	0.4 g
Carbohydrate	3.6 g
Fiber	2.2 g
Folate	194 mcg
Vitamin C	28 mg
Vitamin E	2 mg
Vitamin K	482 mcg
Iron	2.7 mg
Magnesium	79 mg
Potassium	558 mg
Lutein/Zeaxanthin	12,198 mcg
Beta-carotene	5,626 mcg

Researchers have found many flavonoid compounds in spinach that act as antioxidants and fight against stomach, skin, breast, prostate, and other cancers. Spinach is also extremely high in carotenes, which protect eyesight, and is particularly rich in vitamin K, which helps to boost bone strength and may help prevent osteoporosis. It also contains peptides, which have been shown to lower blood pressure. The relatively high vitamin E present may help protect brainpower and memory as we age, while the extremely high amount of folate in spinach offers protection against heart problems, cancers, and birth defects. Spinach is also rich in potassium, magnesium, and iron.

- Flavonoid and carotene content protects against many cancers.
- Vitamin C, folate, and carotenes help maintain heart health.
- Vitamin K and magnesium—important for bone health.
- Extremely rich source of minerals.

Practical tips:
Try to eat spinach with oil to help your body absorb the beneficial carotenes—try stir-frying, drizzle oil over wilted spinach, or add an olive oil and lemon dressing to raw baby leaves. Boost iron absorption by adding plenty of vitamin C-rich foods to your plate.

Spiced chickpea and spinach soup

SERVES 4 Ⓕ Ⓥ Ⓓ Ⓟ Ⓝ

1 tablespoon vegetable oil
1 onion, finely chopped
2 garlic cloves, crushed
1 teaspoon cumin seeds
2 teaspoons medium curry
    powder
1 teaspoon hot chili powder
1 (15-ounce) can chickpeas,
    drained and rinsed
1 (14½-ounce) can diced
    tomatoes
2 cups gluten-free
    vegetable stock
2 cups trimmed,
    chopped spinach
salt and pepper, to taste

Mint dressing
½ cup plain yogurt
2 tablespoons finely chopped
    fresh mint leaves
salt and pepper, to taste

Method

1 Heat the oil in a saucepan over medium heat. Add the onion
   and sauté for 4–5 minutes, or until starting to soften.
2 Add the garlic, cumin seeds, curry powder, and chili powder
   and cook for 1 minute, stirring constantly.
3 Add the chickpeas, tomatoes, and stock and season with salt and
   pepper. Bring to a boil, then reduce the heat, cover, and simmer for
   15 minutes.
4 Meanwhile, to make the mint dressing, mix together the yogurt and
   mint with salt and pepper. Cover and chill until ready to serve.
5 Stir the spinach into the soup and cook for an additional
   1–2 minutes, or until the spinach has wilted. Serve with a little
   of the mint dressing drizzled over the soup.

78 MUSHROOMS

Mushrooms contain several health-boosting compounds that support the immune system and help prevent cancers and arthritis.

Some compounds found in mushrooms are known to help prevent a range of diseases. Dark-gilled and exotic types, such as shiitake, cremini, and porcini, in particular, contain higher levels of these plant chemicals than the paler varieties. Lentinan and canthaxanthin boost the immune system and can help to prevent cancers; autoimmune diseases, such as arthritis and lupus; and infections, such as colds and bronchitis. Their high selenium content is also associated with protection from cancers. Mushrooms are also a useful source of protein for vegetarians and contain high levels of some of the B vitamins, including niacin, potassium to help reduce high blood pressure, and immune-boosting zinc.

- Contain compounds, which can help prevent cancers and autoimmune diseases.
- Rich in the anticancer antioxidant mineral selenium.
- Good source of the B vitamins, including folate and niacin for nerves and energy production.
- Rich in potassium to help reduce high blood pressure.

Practical tips:
Store mushrooms in a paper bag in the refrigerator; don't store them in plastic. Wipe gently to clean, if necessary; if practical, don't peel or remove the stems, because they contain high nutrient levels. Add mushrooms to casseroles, soups, stir-fries, pasta, and rice dishes to increase the nutrient and protein content; stuff and bake larger mushrooms; or serve sliced mushrooms on toast.

DID YOU KNOW?

You should never pick mushrooms growing wild unless you get them checked for safety by a fungi expert. Some harmless varieties look similar to poisonous ones.

NUTRIENTS PER 1½ CUPS/3½ OZ CREMINI MUSHROOMS

Calories	22
Protein	2.5 g
Fat	Trace
Carbohydrate	4.3 g
Fiber	0.6 g
Folate	25 mcg
Niacin	3.8 mg
Calcium	18 mg
Potassium	448 mg
Selenium	26 mcg
Zinc	1.1 mg

Buckwheat, mushrooms, and roasted squash

SERVES 4 （F）（N）

*1 kabocha or butternut squash
(about 2 pounds)*
*1 tablespoon thick balsamic
vinegar*
½ cup olive oil
large pat of butter
*1⅓ cups roasted buckwheat,
rinsed*
1 egg, lightly beaten
*2 cups hot gluten-free
vegetable stock*
1 onion, halved and sliced
*3½ cups quartered small
cremini mushrooms*
2 tablespoons lemon juice
*⅓ cup chopped fresh
flat-leaf parsley*
¼ cup coarsely chopped walnuts
salt and pepper, to taste

Method

1 Preheat the oven to 400°F. Cut the squash into eight wedges, peel, and seed.

2 Put the squash into a roasting pan and toss with the vinegar and ⅓ cup of the oil. Season well with salt and pepper and dot with the butter. Roast in the preheated oven for 25–30 minutes, until slightly caramelized.

3 Meanwhile, put the buckwheat into a skillet. Add the egg, stirring to coat the grains. Stir over medium heat for 3 minutes, until the egg moisture has evaporated. Add the stock and ½ teaspoon of salt. Simmer for 9–10 minutes, until the grains are tender but not disintegrating. Remove from the heat and set aside.

4 Heat the remaining oil in the skillet. Add the onion and sauté over medium heat for 10 minutes. Season with salt and pepper. Add the mushrooms and sauté for 5 minutes. Stir in the buckwheat, lemon juice, and most of the parsley.

5 Transfer the buckwheat mixture to four plates and arrange the squash on top. Sprinkle with the walnuts and the remaining parsley. Serve immediately.

79

GARLIC

Garlic, used as a herb and medicine for thousands of years, is antibiotic and protective against digestive problems, heart disease, and cancer.

Garlic, a member of the same allium family as onions, leeks, and chives, is often used in small quantities, but it can still make a great impact on health. It is rich in allicin, diallyl sulfide, and ajoene—three sulfur compounds that are the main source of its health benefits. Research has found that garlic can help minimize the risk of both blood clots and arterial disease, and many types of cancer. It is also a powerful antibiotic, useful for helping battle infections in the intestine, and can also help cure fungal infections, such as athlete's foot. It also appears to reduce the risk of stomach ulcers. Garlic is a useful source of the antioxidant vitamin C and also contains a little selenium, potassium, and calcium.

- Regular consumption can help prevent heart disease.
- May significantly reduce the risk of colon, stomach, and prostate cancers.
- Naturally antibiotic, antiviral, and antifungal.
- Can help prevent stomach ulcers.

Practical tips:
Crush or chop fresh garlic and let stand for a few minutes before cooking to maximize the protective effects. Tests reveal that short cooking at low temperatures retains more beneficial compounds than longer, higher cooking. Chew fresh parsley after a garlic-rich meal to help avoid garlicky breath.

DID YOU KNOW?

Meat cooked at high temperatures, such as grilling or broiling, can be carcinogenic (cancer-promoting), but adding garlic, in a marinade, for example, reduces the production of carcinogenic chemicals.

NUTRIENTS PER 2 FRESH MEDIUM CLOVES

Calories	9
Protein	0.4 g
Fat	Trace
Carbohydrate	2 g
Fiber	Trace
Vitamin C	2 mg
Calcium	11 mg
Potassium	24 mg

Salmon fish cakes with garlic mayonnaise

MAKES 8   (D) (N)

12 ounces cooked salmon,
    flaked
1½ cups mashed potatoes
½ cup chopped fresh dill, plus
    extra sprigs to garnish
6 scallions, some green part
    included, finely chopped
1 tablespoon coarsely grated
    lemon zest
1 tablespoon cornstarch, sifted
1 teaspoon salt
½ teaspoon pepper
2 eggs, lightly beaten
a little gluten-free all-purpose
    flour, for dusting
vegetable oil, for frying

Garlic mayonnaise
3 large garlic cloves, peeled
1 teaspoon sea salt flakes
2 egg yolks, at room temperature
1 cup extra virgin olive oil
2 tablespoons lemon juice

Method

1 In a large bowl, combine the salmon, potato, dill, scallions, and
   lemon zest, mixing lightly with a fork. Sprinkle with the cornstarch,
   salt, and pepper, then stir in the beaten egg. With floured hands,
   form into eight patties about ¾ inch thick. Place on a parchment
   paper-lined baking sheet and chill for at least 2 hours.

2 To make the garlic mayonnaise, crush the garlic cloves with the sea
   salt, using a mortar and pestle, to make a smooth paste. Transfer
   to a large bowl. Beat in the egg yolks. Add the oil, a few drops at
   a time, whisking constantly, until the mixture is thick and smooth.
   Beat in the lemon juice. Transfer to a serving bowl, cover with
   plastic wrap, and set aside.

3 Heat the oil in a skillet and cook the fish cakes over medium–high
   heat for 8 minutes, until golden. Turn and cook the other side
   for 4–5 minutes, until golden. Garnish with dill sprigs and serve
   immediately with the garlic mayonnaise.

80 CHILES

Hot chiles are one of our favorite spices and can make a much larger contribution to your nutritional health than their size might indicate.

Chiles' main use in cooking—their heat—is also one of their main sources of health-giving properties. Capsaicin is what gives chiles this heat, and this highly beneficial compound relieves the pain and inflammation associated with arthritis. It also appears to block the production of cancerous cells in cases of prostate cancer and acts as an anticoagulant, thus helping protect against blood clots, heart attack, or stroke. It can even ease nasal and lung congestion. Recent research shows that chile consumption helps to lower the amount of insulin required to lower blood sugar after a meal and so could help diabetics and people who are insulin-resistant. This useful spice can also lower LDL cholesterol in the blood.

• Contain capsaicin to relieve pain and inflammation associated with arthritis.
• Strongly antioxidant to help beat prostate cancer and the diseases of aging.
• Help lower LDL cholesterol.
• Rich in vitamin C and carotenes to boost the immune system.

Practical tips:
In general, the hotter the chile the more capsaicin it contains—the hottest varieties include habanero, Thai, and Scotch bonnet. Jalapeños are mid-heat while Hungarian hot wax are mild. Removing the seeds from fresh chiles before use makes them milder but also removes some of the antioxidants. Be careful to avoid rubbing your eyes when preparing chiles.

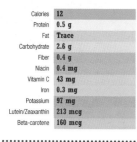

DID YOU KNOW?

Native to Central and South America, chiles have been cultivated for more than 7,000 years—originally as a herbal medicine. After eating chiles, the body's metabolic rate rises, meaning you burn more calories.

NUTRIENTS PER MEDIUM HOT RED CHILE

Calories	12
Protein	0.5 g
Fat	Trace
Carbohydrate	2.6 g
Fiber	0.4 g
Niacin	0.4 mg
Vitamin C	43 mg
Iron	0.3 mg
Potassium	97 mg
Lutein/Zeaxanthin	213 mcg
Beta-carotene	160 mcg

Thai tofu cakes with chili dip

SERSE 4   (N)

12 ounces firm tofu, drained
weight, coarsely grated
1 lemongrass stalk, finely
chopped
2 garlic cloves, chopped
1-inch piece fresh ginger, peeled
and grated
2 kaffir lime leaves, finely
chopped (optional)
2 shallots, finely chopped
2 fresh red chiles, seeded and
finely chopped
¼ cup chopped fresh cilantro
¾ cup gluten-free all-purpose
flour, plus extra for dusting
½ teaspoon salt
vegetable oil, for pan-frying

Chili dip

3 tablespoons white
distilled vinegar
2 scallions, finely sliced
1 tablespoon sugar
2 fresh red chiles, seeded
and chopped
2 tablespoons chopped
fresh cilantro
pinch of salt

Method

1 To make the chili dip, mix all the ingredients together in a small
serving bowl and set aside.

2 Mix the tofu with the lemongrass, garlic, ginger, lime leaves (if
using), shallots, chiles, and cilantro in a mixing bowl. Stir in the
flour and salt to make a coarse, sticky paste. Cover and chill in
the refrigerator for 1 hour to let the mixture become slightly firm.

3 Form the mixture into eight large, walnut-size balls and, using
floured hands, flatten into circles. Heat enough oil to cover the
bottom of a large, heavy skillet over medium heat. Cook the tofu
cakes in two batches, turning halfway through, for 4–6 minutes,
or until golden brown. Drain on paper towels and serve warm
with the chili dip.

81 GINGER

While ginger is a favorite cooking spice, its unique plant compounds are also powerful against inflammation and digestive upsets, making it particularly useful for people recently diagnosed with gluten intolerance.

The most well-researched compounds in ginger are the gingerols, which give it much of its flavor and aroma. These can actually destroy colon, rectal, and ovarian cancer cells. Gingerols also have a powerful anti-inflammatory action and improve pain, swelling, and mobility in up to 75 percent of people with arthritis. Ginger has long been used as a remedy for nausea, morning sickness, and seasickness, and it is also an aid to digestion, relaxing the intestines and helping to eliminate gas. Also present are terpenes, compounds that help keep the blood vessels dilated and can help lower blood pressure and prevent blood clots. Ginger may also ease migraines.

- Proven relief from the pain of arthritis.
- Strong anticancer action.
- Helps keep blood vessels healthy.
- Digestive aid.

Practical tips:
Fresh ginger contains the highest levels of beneficial compounds. Store in the refrigerator and peel and chop or grate as required. Ginger marries well with pears and rhubarb for a fruit compote or add to casseroles, stews, stir-fries, and soups. Or make ginger tea—steep 1 teaspoon grated ginger in hot water for 5 minutes.

DID YOU KNOW?

Ginger is a rhizome—a type of root—used medicinally and as a spice for at least 5,000 years across Asia before arriving in Europe around 2,000 years ago.

NUTRIENTS PER 1 TABLESPOON FRESH CHOPPED GINGER

Calories	19
Protein	0.5 g
Fat	0.3 g
Carbohydrate	3.8 g
Fiber	0.7 g
Iron	0.6 mg
Magnesium	10 mg
Potassium	73 mg

Gingered carrot and pomegranate salad

SERVES 4 (**F**) (**V**) (**D**) (**N**)

3 cups shredded carrots
2-inch piece of fresh ginger,
   peeled and finely grated
1 small pomegranate, quartered
1 cup alfalfa sprouts or
   radish sprouts

Dressing

3 tablespoons light olive oil
1 tablespoon red wine vinegar
1 tablespoon pomegranate
   molasses
salt and pepper, to taste

Method

1 Put the carrots and ginger in a salad bowl. Flex the pomegranate pieces to pop out the seeds, prying any stubborn ones out with the tip of a small knife, and add to the bowl.

2 To make the dressing, put the oil, vinegar, and pomegranate molasses in a clean screw-top jar, season with salt and pepper, screw on the lid, and shake well. Drizzle the dressing over the salad and toss gently together. Cover and let marinate in the refrigerator for 30 minutes.

3 Sprinkle the sprouts over the salad and serve.

6

Meat, fish, and dairy

Each delicious food in this chapter has something special to offer for nutrition and health. Lean meats, such as beef and venison, are packed with high-quality protein and the B vitamins, which can be in short supply on a gluten-free diet, and high levels of iron for energy. Oily fish are rich in those hard-to-get omega-3 fats for heart health, while shellfish boast plenty of immune-boosting zinc. Cheese is one of our best sources of calcium, while yogurt is ideal for a sensitive digestive tract, and eggs are rich in almost every vitamin and mineral you can name.

(C) High in carbohydrate

(F) Good source of fiber

(V) Rich in vitamins and minerals

(D) Particularly good for digestive health

(P) High in protein

(N) Nutrient boost for gluten-free diet

82

CHICKEN

Lean chicken meat is one of the best protein choices you can make, because it provides an impressive range of nutrients and compounds to boost your health.

Both chicken breast and leg meat are nutrient rich, but while the breast is lower in fat and saturates, the darker leg meat is higher in iron and zinc. Chicken is high in niacin (vitamin B_3) and choline, another B vitamin—both of these help to lower LDL cholesterol and homocysteine in the blood, providing protection against cardiovascular disease. Chicken is high in the antioxidant mineral selenium, shown to help protect us from cancer, and it is a good source of iron, which helps transport oxygen around the body. It is also rich in zinc, a powerful immune booster. Chicken soup really is good for you—it contains a compound called carnosine, which helps to fight colds and flu, and cystine, an antibiotic.

- Rich in the B vitamins to protect the heart and circulation.
- Excellent source of zinc, an immune-boosting mineral.
- Proved to contain natural antibiotic and immune-boosting compounds.

Practical tips:
Try to buy organic meat, which contains more omega-3 fats and vitamin E. When preparing raw chicken, wash hands and utensils thoroughly afterward and use a dedicated cutting board. Use the chicken carcass for soups, stocks, and stews, because the bones have the greatest immune-boosting effect. Make sure chicken is thoroughly cooked with no pink flesh.

DID YOU KNOW?

Chicken livers are rich in iron and vitamin B_{12}, both of which can be lacking in a gluten-free diet.

NUTRIENTS PER 3½ oz LEAN CHICKEN BREAST (SKIN REMOVED)

Calories	114
Protein	21 g
Fat	2.6 g
Vitamin B6	0.7 mg
Vitamin B_{12}	0.2 mcg
Choline	73 mg
Niacin	10.4 mg
Calcium	5 mg
Iron	0.5 mg
Magnesium	26 mg
Phosphorous	210 mg
Potassium	370 mg
Selenium	32 mcg
Zinc	0.6 mg

Chicken tacos

SERVES 4   (v) (P)

1 ripe avocado
⅔ cup plain yogurt
2 tablespoons medium cornmeal
1 teaspoon chili powder
½ teaspoon dried thyme
1¼ pounds skinless, boneless
   chicken breasts, cut into
   thin strips
2 tablespoons sunflower oil
1 red onion, sliced
1 large red bell pepper,
   seeded and sliced
1 large green bell pepper,
   seeded and sliced
8 gluten-free taco shells
salt and pepper, to taste
smoked paprika, to garnish

Method

1 Halve the avocado, remove the pit, and scoop out the flesh, then puree in a blender with the yogurt. Season with salt and pepper.

2 Mix together the cornmeal, chili powder, and thyme with salt and pepper in a large bowl. Add the chicken and toss to coat evenly.

3 Heat the oil in a wok or large skillet and stir-fry the onion and bell peppers for 3–4 minutes, until softened. Remove from the pan and keep hot.

4 Add the chicken and stir-fry for 5–6 minutes, until evenly browned. Return the vegetables to the pan and stir-fry for an additional 1–2 minutes.

5 Spoon the chicken mixture into the taco shells and top with a spoonful of the avocado mixture. Sprinkle with smoked paprika and serve.

83 TURKEY

Turkey is becoming more popular to eat year-round and its excellent health credentials make this versatile meat a sensible choice in a gluten-free diet.

Turkey breast contains less fat than any other meat and its high protein content means it is ideal for those watching their weight and for diabetics, because tests show it is a type of protein that can regulate insulin production. Turkey is surprisingly rich in vitamins and minerals. The light meat, the most popular type eaten by far, is a good source of vitamin B6 and iron, while the dark meat is an even better source of most of the minerals. For example, 3½ ounces of lean turkey leg meat has a whopping 3.2 mg of zinc—nearly half your RDA in a large slice. High in both potassium and phosphorous, turkey is an ideal food for helping to reduce high blood pressure and maintaining healthy bones and teeth.

- Low in fat and high in nutrient-rich protein, which helps to regulate insulin.
- Good source of many of the B vitamins, particularly B6.
- Turkey leg meat is a good source of immune-boosting zinc.
- Phosphorous content helps maintain bones and teeth.

Practical tips:
Turkey can be used in almost any recipe where you would use chicken or pork. Ground leg meat makes a good substitute for beef in burgers, meatballs, or chili. If cooking a whole turkey, cook any stuffing separately to be sure that it and the bird are cooked properly all the way through.

DID YOU KNOW?

Meat from turkeys that graze on natural pasture contains a little more fat, including some omega-3 fats, and more carotenes than meat from penned turkeys.

NUTRIENTS PER 3½ oz TURKEY BREAST (SKIN REMOVED)

Calories	115
Protein	23.5 g
Fat	1.6 g
Vitamin B5	0.7 mg
Vitamin B6	0.6 mg
Vitamin B12	0.5 mcg
Niacin	5.8 mg
Vitamin D	0.3 mcg
Iron	1.2 mg
Magnesium	27 mg
Phosphorous	204 mg
Potassium	305 mg
Selenium	24.5 mcg
Zinc	1.6 mg

Turkey, rice and cranberry salad

SERVES 4 (**V**) (**P**) (**N**)

¾ cup brown rice

¼ cup wild rice

8 ounces turkey breast cutlets

⅓ cup dried cranberries

3 scallions, finely chopped

2 tomatoes, diced

1 small red bell pepper, halved,
    seeded, and cut into chunks

2 cups arugula

2 ounces gluten-free,
    wafer-thin sliced, cooked
    ham, cut into strips

salt and pepper, to taste

Dressing

1½ tablespoons cranberry sauce

1½ tablespoons sherry vinegar

finely grated zest and juice
    of 1 small lemon

1 teaspoon gluten-free
    Dijon mustard

salt and pepper, to taste

Method

1 Put cold water in the bottom of a steamer, bring to a boil, then
   add the brown rice and wild rice and bring back to a boil. Put the
   turkey in the top of the steamer in a single layer, season with salt
   and pepper, then put it on the steamer base, cover, and steam for
   15 minutes, or until the turkey is cooked; cut into the middle of a
   slice to check that the meat is no longer pink and that the juices are
   clear and piping hot. Remove the steamer top and cook the rice for
   an additional 5–10 minutes, or until tender.

2 Dice the turkey and put it in a bowl. Add the cranberries. Drain and
   rinse the rice, then add to the bowl.

3 To make the dressing, put the cranberry sauce into a small
   saucepan over low heat until just melted. Remove from the heat,
   then add the vinegar, lemon zest and juice, mustard, and a little
   salt and pepper. Whisk together until smooth, then drizzle over the
   salad and let cool.

4 Add the scallions, tomatoes, and red pepper to the salad. Toss
   gently together, then divide among four plates. Top with the arugula
   and ham and serve.

84 DUCK

Duck has amazingly diverse and high levels of vitamins and minerals and is an extremely healthy meat, rich in high-quality complete protein.

NUTRIENTS PER 3½ oz DUCK (SKIN REMOVED)

Calories	135
Protein	18.2 g
Fat	6 g
Vitamin A	29 mcg
Vitamin B$_1$	0.4 mg
Vitamin B$_2$	0.5 mg
Vitamin B$_5$	1.6 mg
Vitamin B$_6$	0.3 mg
Vitamin B$_{12}$	0.4 mcg
Choline	53.6 mg
Folate	25 mcg
Niacin	5.3 mg
Iron	2.4 mg
Magnesium	19 mg
Potassium	271 mg
Selenium	13.9 mcg
Zinc	1.9 mg

Duck with its skin and fat left on contains around 28 percent fat, but over half of this is the healthy, unsaturated type. And with the fat trimmed, the bird is, in fact, a relatively lean, high-protein meat at around only 6 g fat per 3½ ounces. It is an especially rich source of selenium and zinc—important antioxidant minerals that protect against disease and the signs of aging. Selenium has anticancer and thyroid-boosting properties, while zinc is a strong immune-booster. Duck is rich in the B vitamins, which support the nervous system and help keep your heart healthy. The B vitamin choline is powerfully anti-inflammatory and can also help minimize the symptoms of arthritis.

• Contains vitamins and antioxidants for heart protection.
• Rich in a range of important minerals.
• High in the vitamin-B group, including anti-inflammatory choline.
• High in potassium to regulate blood pressure.

Practical tips:
Wild duck has an even higher proportion of mono- and polyunsaturated fats (around two-thirds) than farmed duck and is a leaner bird altogether. Duck goes particularly well with peas, beans, broccoli, oranges, apples, and cherries. Anyone with a weakened immune system, the elderly, infants, and pregnant women should avoid eating undercooked (pink) duck meat. Pierce the thickest part of the meat to check that the juices are clear and no longer pink.

Duck breasts with plum sauce

SERVES 4 (V) (D) (P) (N)

*1 tablespoon duck fat or
    sunflower oil*
*4 duck breasts, about 12 ounces
    each, finely scored through
    the skin to the fat*
cooked green beans, to serve

Plum sauce

1 tablespoon sunflower oil
1 shallot, finely chopped
*1½ tablespoons light brown
    sugar, plus extra, if needed*
½ teaspoon ground ginger
*4 plums, pitted and coarsely
    chopped*
¼ cup gluten-free dry white wine
*1 teaspoon orange juice,
    plus extra, if needed*
salt and pepper, to taste

Method

1 Preheat the oven to 400°F. To make the sauce, heat the oil in a
    skillet over high heat. Add the shallot and cook until soft. Stir in the
    sugar and ginger, add the plums, and season with salt and pepper.
    Stir until the sugar is dissolved and is just beginning to caramelize.
    Immediately add the wine and orange juice and bring to a boil,
    stirring. Reduce the heat to low and let simmer until the plums are
    tender and beginning to fall apart and the liquid is reduced. Taste
    and adjust the seasoning with salt and pepper, if needed. Add extra
    sugar or orange juice, depending on how tart or sweet the plums
    are. Cover the sauce and set aside until required.

2 Meanwhile, melt the duck fat or oil in a large, flameproof casserole
    or Dutch oven wide enough to hold all the breasts in a single layer,
    or use a large skillet with an ovenproof handle. Add the duck
    breasts, skin side down, and cook for 3–5 minutes, or until golden
    brown. Turn the duck breasts skin side up and put them in the oven
    for 10 minutes for medium-rare and up to 15 minutes for well done.
    Transfer the duck breasts to a cutting board, cover, and let rest for
    5 minutes.

3 Thinly slice the duck breasts diagonally and transfer to warm
    plates. Add any accumulated juices to the sauce and quickly return
    the sauce to a boil to reheat. Serve immediately, with the sauce
    spooned over the duck breasts and the green beans alongside.

85 PORK

Pork is a particularly nutrient-rich meat. It is full of first-class protein, zinc, phosphorus, selenium, potassium, and almost all the B vitamins.

A 3½-ounce serving of pork provides around two-thirds of your RDA for vitamin B_1, the B vitamin necessary for converting carbohydrates into energy and essential for muscle growth and repair. Its high levels of vitamins B_2 and niacin help to regulate energy release throughout the day. Pork is rich in two minerals that strengthen your bones—phosphorus and magnesium—and provides one-quarter of your RDA for zinc to bolster your immune system and help promote healthy new cells throughout your body. The same serving size of pork will also give you more than half of your daily needs of the antioxidant mineral selenium.

- High in top-quality protein to build and maintain muscle bulk and strength.
- Good source of a wide range of the B vitamins.
- High in bone-building minerals.
- One of the best sources of zinc for a healthy immune system.

Practical tips:
Pork tenderloin is an ideal cut to buy, because it is extremely lean and tender. All pork should be thoroughly cooked with no pink left when you serve. Ground pork can be substituted for beef or lamb in almost any recipe. This meat goes well with green and red cabbage, rosemary, and apples.

DID YOU KNOW?

Nearly half the fat in lean pork is the healthy mono-unsaturated kind—like that in olive oil—while only one-third is saturated.

NUTRIENTS PER 3½ oz LEAN PORK

Calories	143
Protein	21.5 g
Fat	5.6 g
Vitamin B_1	1 mg
Vitamin B_2	0.3 mg
Vitamin B_5	0.8 mg
Vitamin B_6	0.5 mg
Vitamin B_{12}	0.6 mcg
Choline	75.6 mg
Niacin	4.9 mg
Vitamin D	0.5 mcg
Iron	0.8 mg
Magnesium	23 mg
Phosphorous	211 mg
Potassium	389 mg
Selenium	36 mcg
Zinc	1.8 mg

Roasted pork with gingered apples

SERVES 4 (V) (P) (N)

2 garlic cloves, crushed
¼ cup gluten-free red wine
2 tablespoons packed light
  brown sugar
1 tablespoon gluten-free tamari
  (Japanese soy sauce)
1 teaspoon sesame oil
½ teaspoon ground cinnamon
¼ teaspoon ground cloves
1 star anise, broken into
  pieces
½ teaspoon pepper
12 ounces pork tenderloin
cooked green beans,
  to serve

Gingered apples
4 Granny Smith or other cooking
  apples, coarsely chopped
1 tablespoon rice vinegar
1 tablespoon packed light
  brown sugar
¼ cup apple juice
1 tablespoon finely chopped
  fresh ginger

Method

1 In a large bowl, combine the garlic, wine, brown sugar, tamari,
   sesame oil, cinnamon, cloves, star anise, and pepper. Add the pork
   and toss to coat. Cover and refrigerate overnight.

2 Preheat the oven to 375°F. Heat a nonstick skillet over high heat.
   Remove the pork from the marinade and sear in the hot pan.
   Cook for about 8 minutes, or until browned on all sides. Transfer
   the pork to an ovenproof dish and drizzle with half the marinade.
   Roast in the preheated oven for 15 minutes. Turn the meat, drizzle
   the remaining marinade over the top, and roast for an additional
   30 minutes, or until cooked through (insert the tip of a sharp knife
   into the center of the pork and check that there is no pink meat).

3 Meanwhile, make the gingered apples. In a saucepan, combine
   all the ingredients and cook over medium–high heat until the liquid
   begins to boil. Reduce the heat to medium–low and simmer, stirring
   occasionally, for about 20 minutes, or until the apples are soft.

4 Remove the pork from the oven and set aside to rest for 5 minutes.
   Slice the meat and serve with the apples and green beans.

86 BEEF

Lean beef contains top-quality protein and is a vitamin B-rich, energy-giving, low-fat food perfect for a gluten-free diet.

Few people realize that lean beef is one of the lower-fat, lower-saturates meats with a high protein percentage, and as such is a useful food for a healthy balanced diet. It is one of the best sources of the B vitamins, which have a variety of roles to play within your body. The B vitamins are among the most important vitamins for the nervous system and in converting the food you eat into energy. They also provide cardiovascular protection. Beef contains valuable levels of many minerals and is a particularly good source of easily absorbed iron to prevent anemia and fatigue. In addition, an average 4½-ounce serving provides nearly half of your RDA of the immunity-boosting zinc.

- Low-fat and rich in high-quality complete protein.
- Rich in the B vitamins.
- High in iron for healthy blood and protection against fatigue.
- Great source of zinc.

Practical tips:
The less expensive cuts of beef, such as shin, are the best cuts for slow-cooking dishes, such as casseroles and stews—simply cook the day before, refrigerate, then remove any solidified fat from the top before reheating. Top cuts, such as tenderloin and sirloin, need to be cooked minimally to retain the vitamin B-rich juices. Make beef go farther by using in soups and recipes with beans and gluten-free grains, such as chili con carne.

DID YOU KNOW?

Pasture-raised beef, from animals that have eaten mostly grass and herbs, will offer extra nutritional benefit and contain high levels of omega-3 fats, vitamin E, and carotenes.

NUTRIENTS PER 3½ oz LEAN BEEF

Calories	117
Protein	23 g
Fat	2.7 g
Vitamin B$_6$	1.3 mg
Vitamin B$_{12}$	9 mcg
Choline	65 mg
Niacin	6.7 mg
Calcium	0.6 mg
Iron	1.8 mg
Magnesium	23 mg
Phosphorous	212 mg
Potassium	342 mg
Selenium	21 mcg
Zinc	3.6 mg

Steak and fries with watercress butter

SERVES 4   (V) (P) (N)

*1 bunch of watercress or argula,
plus extra to garnish*
*6 tablespoons unsalted butter,
softened*
*4 tenderloin steaks or top
loin (strip) steaks, about
8 ounces each*
4 teaspoons hot pepper sauce
salt and pepper, to taste

Fries

4 russet potatoes, peeled
2 tablespoons sunflower oil

Method

1 To make the fries, preheat
the oven to 400°F. Cut the
potatoes into thick, even
sticks. Rinse them under cold
running water and then dry well
on a clean dish towel. Place in
a bowl, add the oil, and toss
together until coated.

2 Spread the fries in a single
layer on a baking sheet and
cook in the preheated oven for
40–45 minutes, turning once,
or until golden.

3 Using a sharp knife, finely
chop enough watercress to
fill ¼ cup. Place the butter in
a small bowl and beat in the
chopped watercress with a
fork until fully incorporated.
Cover with plastic wrap and
let chill in the refrigerator
until required.

4 Preheat a ridged grill pan to
high. Sprinkle each steak with
1 teaspoon of the hot pepper
sauce, rubbing it in well.
Season with salt and pepper.

5 Cook the steaks on the
preheated pan for 2½ minutes
each side for rare, 4 minutes
each side for medium, and
6 minutes each side for well
done. Transfer to serving plates
and serve immediately, topped
with the watercress butter
and accompanied by the fries.
Garnish with watercress.

87 VENISON

Becoming more popular than ever, tender and lean venison meat is packed with iron, zinc, and several other important nutrients vital for a gluten-free diet.

Extremely high in protein and lower in fat than most meats, game, or poultry, venison is gaining in popularity as an alternative to beef because it has a similar richness of flavor and appearance. It is higher in iron than any other meat and is even richer in zinc than turkey leg meat. It also contains a whole day's recommended amount of vitamin B_{12} in a 3½-ounce serving—this vitamin is only present in animal foods, not in vegetables, fruits, or grains. Venison is also extremely high in niacin, which is needed for healthy skin and for the body to convert food to energy. Both B_{12} and niacin are probably in short supply on a gluten-free diet.

- High in top-quality protein that can help the body regulate insulin levels.
- Low in fat.
- Rich in iron for healthy blood and oxygen transportation.
- Contains large amounts of most of the B vitamins, particularly vitamin B_{12}.

Practical tips:
Venison steaks are quick to cook and can be cooked in exactly the same way as beef steaks—brush the sides of the meat with oil, then broil or grill in a dry pan. Cubed venison is ideal for casseroles, and the meat goes particularly well with mushrooms, tomatoes, celery, and chestnuts. Venison freezes well.

DID YOU KNOW?

Venison contains a special type of fat called conjugated linoleic acid (CLA), which is thought to protect us against heart disease and some cancers, including colon cancer, and help to control body weight.

NUTRIENTS PER 3½ oz VENISON

Calories	149
Protein	30 g
Fat	2.4 g
Vitamin B_1	0.3 mg
Vitamin B_2	0.6 mg
Vitamin B_5	0.9 mg
Vitamin B_6	0.6 mg
Vitamin B_{12}	3.6 mcg
Niacin	8.8 mg
Vitamin E	0.6 mg
Iron	4.2 mg
Magnesium	33 mg
Phosphorous	299 mg
Potassium	434 mg
Selenium	11 mcg
Zinc	4 mg

Charbroiled venison steaks

SERVES 4 (V) (P) (N)

4 venison steaks
fresh thyme sprigs, to garnish

Marinade

⅔ cup gluten-free red wine
2 tablespoons olive oil
1 tablespoon red wine vinegar
1 onion, chopped
1 tablespoon each chopped
*   fresh parsley and chopped*
*   fresh thyme*
1 bay leaf
1 teaspoon good-quality honey
½ teaspoon gluten-free mustard
salt and pepper, to taste

Method

1 Place the venison steaks in a shallow, nonmetallic dish.

2 To make the marinade, add the wine, oil, wine vinegar, onion, parsley, thyme, bay leaf, honey, and mustard to a clean screw-top jar and season with salt and pepper. Cover with the lid and shake vigorously until well combined. Alternatively, using a fork, whisk the ingredients together in a bowl.

3 Pour the marinade mixture over the venison, cover, and let marinate in the refrigerator overnight. Turn the steaks over in the mixture occasionally so that the meat is well coated.

4 Preheat the broiler to high. Cook the venison under the hot broiler for 2 minutes on each side to seal the meat.

5 Turn down the broiler to medium, and cook for an additional 4–10 minutes on each side, according to taste. Test the meat by inserting the tip of a sharp knife into the meat—the juices will range from red when the meat is still rare to clear as the meat becomes well cooked.

6 Transfer the steaks to serving plates, garnish with fresh thyme sprigs, and serve.

88

CRAB

Crab is a low-fat, high-protein shellfish containing l-tyrosine for a brain-power boost and high levels of several protective minerals, including selenium and zinc.

A 3½-ounce serving of crab provides more than half a day's recommended selenium intake for an adult. This is a powerful antioxidant mineral with anticancer action. In addition, a similar portion of crab gives you around half your day's RDA for zinc, a mineral that is not only antioxidant but also boosts the immune system and is vital for reproduction, growth, and development. The body produces the amino acid l-tyrosine, but this is a natural food source of the protein that plays an important role in brain function. Crab is also a good source of iron, calcium, and potassium. And the meat is high in folate—a B vitamin that protects against birth defects and is vital for pregnant women. It is also linked to reducing the level of homocysteine in the blood, high levels of which are linked to heart disease.

- High in selenium to protect against cancer.
- Great source of zinc and other minerals.
- Contributes folate and a range of other B vitamins.
- Low in fat and saturates but high in protein.

Practical tips:
Try to buy cooked fresh or frozen crabmeat, because canned crab is often high in sodium. Crab, particularly the nutrient-rich brown flesh, is rich, so serve with simple, fresh flavors, such as lemon.

DID YOU KNOW?

Dressed crab is the name given in the UK to crabmeat that has been cooked and removed from the shell to make it easy to use with no additional preparation.

NUTRIENTS PER 3½ oz DRESSED CRAB (BROWN AND WHITE MEAT)

Calories	128
Protein	19.5 g
Fat	5.5 g
Folate	20 mcg
Niacin	1.5 mg
Calcium	26 mg
Iron	2.5 mg
Magnesium	58 mg
Potassium	250 mg
Selenium	36 mcg
Zinc	5.5 mg

Crab fritters with avocado salsa

SERVES 4 Ⓥ Ⓟ Ⓝ

1⅓ cups lightly cooked
    corn kernels
⅔ cup gluten-free
    all-purpose flour
2 eggs, beaten
12 ounces white crabmeat,
    drained if canned
1 small bunch fresh flat-leaf
    parsley, chopped
3–4 tablespoons olive oil
salt and pepper, to taste
lime wedges, to garnish

Avocado salsa

1 small red onion,
    finely chopped
1 red bell pepper, seeded
    and diced
1 yellow bell pepper, seeded
    and diced
1 avocado, peeled, pitted,
    and diced
1 mango, peeled, pitted,
    and diced
4 tomatoes
juice and finely grated zest
    of 2 limes
1 large bunch fresh cilantro,
    chopped
salt and pepper, to taste

Method

1. To make the avocado salsa, put the onion, bell peppers, avocado, and mango in a bowl. Chop the tomatoes into ½-inch dice and add to the other ingredients. Stir in the lime juice and zest and cilantro. Season with salt and pepper.

2. Next make the fritters—put the corn kernels, flour, and eggs into a separate bowl and stir until well mixed. Lightly fold in the crabmeat and parsley, and season with salt and pepper.

3. Heat the oil in a large skillet over medium–high heat. Drop spoonfuls of the crab fritter mixture into the hot oil and cook in batches for 2–3 minutes on each side, until crisp and golden. Remove and drain on paper towels. Serve immediately with the avocado salsa and the lime wedges for squeezing over the fritters.

89 MUSSELS

Mussels contain a wide range of health-giving minerals and vitamins and, despite being low in fat, are a good source of the essential fatty acids EPA and DHA.

NUTRIENTS PER 3½ oz SHELLED MUSSELS

Calories	86
Protein	11.9 g
Fat	2.2 g
EPA	0.41 g
DHA	0.16 g
Vitamin B$_{12}$	12 mcg
Folate	42 mcg
Vitamin C	8 mg
Vitamin E	0.55 mg
Calcium	26 mg
Iron	3.9 mg
Magnesium	34 mg
Potassium	320 mg
Selenium	44.8 mg
Zinc	1.6 mg

Mussels are low in saturated fat and high in protein, and they also contain some omega-3 essential fats, which are strongly linked with heart and joint health. Unlike some other shellfish, such as shrimp, they are low in cholesterol. They also provide a wide range of vitamins and many minerals in excellent amounts. A 5½-ounce serving of mussels (shelled) will provide around one-third of a day's recommended intake of iron for an adult (for healthy blood) and around three-quarters of a day's selenium requirement (for protection against cancer). They are a good source of the B vitamins, providing more than 100 percent of your RDA for vitamin B$_{12}$ and one-quarter for folate. Mussels are also a helpful source of iodine for healthy thyroid function.

• A low-calorie, low-fat source of complete protein.
• Contain useful amounts of omega-3 essential fats.
• Rich in iron, iodine, zinc, and selenium.
• Good source of the B vitamins.

Practical tips:
If you buy fresh, live mussels, you must prepare and cook them carefully—discard any that don't close tight when tapped. Steam, as per your recipe, for 3–4 minutes, until all the shells are open, and discard any that don't open within a few minutes. You can also buy cooked mussels from the supermarket. Mussels go well with garlic, parsley, and white wine and can be added to fish stews, soups, paella, and shellfish salads.

Mussels in white wine

SERVES 4 Ⓥ Ⓟ Ⓝ

4½ pounds fresh mussels,
  scrubbed and debearded
1¼ cups gluten-free
  dry white wine
6 shallots, finely chopped
1 bouquet garni sachet (sprigs of
  parsley, bay leaf, and thyme
  tied together)
pepper, to taste
fresh flat-leaf parsley sprigs,
  to garnish

Method

1 Discard any mussels with broken shells and any that refuse to close
   when tapped.
2 Pour the wine into a large, heavy saucepan, add the shallots
   and bouquet garni, and season with pepper. Bring to a boil over
   medium heat, add the mussels, and cover tightly. Cook, shaking
   the saucepan occasionally, for 3–4 minutes, or until the mussels
   have opened. Remove and discard the bouquet garni and any
   mussels that remain closed.
3 Using a slotted spoon, divide the mussels among individual serving
   dishes. Tilt the saucepan to let any sand settle, then spoon the
   cooking liquid over the mussels. Garnish with parsley sprigs and
   serve immediately.

90 SCALLOPS

Scallops are a treat that is also good for you—these shellfish boost your vitamin B_{12}, which can be low if you're following a gluten-free diet, and magnesium and can protect your arteries and bone health.

Scallops are an excellent source of vitamin B_{12}, needed by our bodies for several functions, including the deactivation of homocysteine, a chemical that can damage blood vessel walls, and for healthy blood cell and nerve formation. High homocysteine levels are also linked with osteoporosis, and a recent study found that osteoporosis occurred more frequently among women whose vitamin B_{12} status was deficient. A high intake of vitamin B_{12} can also help protect against colon cancer. Scallops are a good source of magnesium, a regular intake of which helps build bone, release energy, regulate nerves, and keep the heart healthy. They are also rich in tryptophan, an amino acid that boosts production of serotonin in our brains, linked with improved mood and relaxation.

- Low in calories and fat.
- Rich in magnesium, which has several roles to play in body maintenance.
- A good source of vitamin B_{12} for a variety of health benefits.
- Good source of minerals, including immune-boosting zinc and potassium for blood pressure regulation.

Practical tips:
Scallops need cooking for only a few minutes or they will become chewy. The sweet flavor of scallops goes well with chile, cilantro, garlic, and parsley, as well as lentils, peas, and bacon.

DID YOU KNOW?

Scallops are an animal, not a fish. They are mollusks, and the part that we eat is the muscle that helps the animal swim and to open and close its shell.

NUTRIENTS PER 3½ oz SHELLED SCALLOPS

Calories	106
Protein	16.2 g
Fat	3 g
Vitamin B_{12}	1.5 mcg
Folate	16 mcg
Calcium	24 mg
Magnesium	56 mg
Potassium	280 mg
Selenium	22 mcg
Zinc	0.95 mg

Scallops with pea puree

SERVES 4　(F)(V)(D)(P)(N)

3 cups frozen peas

2 large handfuls fresh mint
　leaves, coarsely chopped

1 stick plus 3 tablespoons butter

12 fat scallops, roes attached, if
　possible, and removed from
　their shells

salt and pepper, to taste

Method

1　Bring a large saucepan of water to a boil, then add the peas. Bring
　back to a boil and simmer for 3 minutes. Drain the peas, then put
　them in a food processor or blender with the mint, the stick of
　butter, and a large pinch of salt. Process to a smooth puree, adding
　a little hot water if the mixture needs loosening. Taste for seasoning,
　cover, and keep warm.

2　Pat the scallops dry, then season them well with salt and pepper.
　Place a large skillet over high heat and add the remaining butter.
　When the butter starts to smoke, add the scallops and sear them
　for 1–2 minutes on each side. They should be brown and crisp
　on the outside but light and moist in the middle. Remove the
　pan from the heat.

3　Spread a spoonful of pea puree on each of four plates and place
　three scallops on top of each. Season and serve immediately.

91

SQUID

Rich in protein, yet low in calories and fat, and with an abundance of the useful B vitamins and minerals that can be low in a gluten-free diet, squid is one of the most useful seafoods to include in your diet.

DID YOU KNOW?

When a squid is threatened in the wild, it often releases an inky-looking substance that we call squid ink. This is used in Mediterranean cooking to add color and flavor to some dishes. There is evidence emerging that the ink may help prevent some cancers.

NUTRIENTS PER 3½ oz FRESH SQUID (EDIBLE PORTION)

Calories	92
Protein	16 g
Fat	1.4 g
Vitamin B$_2$	0.4 mg
Vitamin B$_5$	0.5 mg
Vitamin B$_{12}$	1.3 mcg
Niacin	2.2 mg
Calcium	32 mg
Iron	0.7 mg
Magnesium	33 mg
Potassium	246 mg
Selenium	44.8 mcg
Zinc	1.5 mg

Containing the whole range of the B vitamins, with a particularly high concentration of vitamins B$_2$, B$_3$, B$_5$, and B$_{12}$, squid is also a good source of several minerals, including the antioxidant selenium, the immune boosters iron and zinc, and potassium, which helps to regulate blood pressure. Squid is a useful source of calcium and magnesium – both help bone strength and regulate the heartbeat, and calcium is a relaxant, helping beat insomnia. Higher in protein than many other types of fish, squid is a useful food to include in your diet if you are watching your weight, because it is so low in calories. Squid even contains a small but useful amount of the omega-3 fats EPA and DHA, important for heart health.

- High in the B vitamins.
- Rich in many minerals, including selenium, iron, and zinc.
- Contains calcium and magnesium to aid bone and heart health.
- High protein, low fat, and low calorie.

Practical tips:

Once cleaned and cut into strips, squid is quick and easy to cook. Be careful to avoid overcooking, because this toughens it. Squid can be served hot—for example, as part of a fish soup or Spanish paella—or added to salads. Frozen squid retains the vitamins and minerals of fresh.

Calamari with shrimp and fava beans

SERVES 4–6 (**V**) (**P**) (**N**)

2 tablespoons olive oil

4 scallions, thinly sliced

2 garlic cloves, finely chopped

1 pound cleaned squid bodies,
  thickly sliced

½ cup gluten-free dry white wine

1½ cups fresh or frozen baby
  fava beans

8 ounces raw jumbo shrimp,
  peeled and deveined

¼ cup chopped fresh
  flat-leaf parsley

salt and pepper, to taste

Method

1 Heat the oil in a large skillet with a lid, add the scallions, and cook over medium heat, stirring occasionally, for 4–5 minutes, until soft.

2 Add the garlic and cook, stirring, for 30 seconds, until soft.

3 Add the squid and cook over high heat, stirring occasionally, for 2 minutes, or until golden brown.

4 Stir in the wine and bring to a boil. Add the beans, reduce the heat, cover, and simmer for 5–8 minutes, if using fresh beans, or 4–5 minutes, if using frozen beans, until tender.

5 Add the shrimp, replace the lid, and simmer for an additional 2–3 minutes, until the shrimp turn pink and start to curl.

6 Stir in the chopped parsley and season with salt and pepper. Serve immediately.

92 SEA BASS

While sea bass is classed as a white fish, it contains several nutrients more commonly associated with oily fish or shellfish and will boost your intake of nutrients sometimes lacking in a gluten-free diet.

NUTRIENTS PER 3½ oz FRESH SEA BASS

Calories	97
Protein	18.4 g
Fat	2 g
EPA	0.2 g
DHA	0.4 g
Vitamin A	46 mcg
Vitamin B5	0.8 mg
Vitamin B6	0.4 mg
Vitamin B12	0.3 mcg
Choline	60.8 mg
Niacin	1.6 mg
Vitamin D	5.6 mcg
Vitamin E	0.8 mg
Magnesium	41 mg
Phosphorous	194 mg
Potassium	256 mg
Selenium	36 mcg
Zinc	0.4 mg

Sea bass is one of the few fish classed in the "white fish" category to contain useful amounts of the long-chain fats EPA and DHA, found only in fish (more usually in oily fish, such as salmon). One-third of sea bass's total fat content is these omega-3 fats, and one 3½-ounce serving will give you more than a day's recommended intake to help prevent cardiovascular disease. The fish also boasts a long list of vitamins and minerals and is a particularly good source of most of the B vitamins, including vitamin B_{12}, which we need on a daily basis because it is a water-soluble vitamin and not stored in the body. It also contains an impressive amount of the anticancer, antioxidant mineral selenium.

- Higher in omega-3 EPA and DHA fats than most other white fish.
- Good source of vitamins A, D, and E and most of the B vitamins.
- Rich in a broad spectrum of minerals, including phosphorous and magnesium for heart and bone health.
- Good source of selenium.

Practical tips:
Sea bass has a delicate yet distinctive flavor and a fine texture and is becoming one of the most popular fish to eat across the world. Whole fish can be baked or pan fried, fillets can be steamed, grilled, or broiled, and all cuts can be wrapped in parchment paper with flavorings and cooked *en papillote*, or as a package. Eat or freeze on the day you buy it.

Baked sea bass with white bean puree

SERVES 4 (F) (V) (P)

2 tablespoons olive oil
1 tablespoon fresh thyme leaves
4 large sea bass fillets, about
   6 ounces each
salt and pepper, to taste
cherry tomatoes, to serve

White bean puree

3 tablespoons olive oil
2 garlic cloves, chopped
2 (15½-ounce) cans cannellini
   or lima beans, drained
   and rinsed
juice of 1 lemon
2–3 tablespoons water
¼ cup chopped fresh
   flat-leaf parsley
salt and pepper, to taste

Method

1 Preheat the oven to 400°F. Mix together the oil, thyme, salt and pepper in a small bowl. Arrange the sea bass fillets on a baking pan, pour the oil mixture over the fish, and carefully turn to coat well. Put the pan on the top shelf of the preheated oven and bake for 15 minutes.

2 Meanwhile, make the white bean puree. Heat the oil in a saucepan over medium heat, add the garlic, and cook, stirring, for 1 minute. Add the beans and heat through for 3–4 minutes, then add the lemon juice and season with salt and pepper. Transfer to a food processor or blender, add the water, and process lightly until you have a puree. Alternatively, mash thoroughly with a fork. Stir the parsley into the puree.

3 Serve the sea bass fillets immediately, on top of the warm white bean puree with a drizzle of any pan juices and the cherry tomatoes.

93

SALMON

Salmon is an excellent source of the essential omega-3 fats and is rich in a range of the B vitamins, making it an ideal fish for a gluten-free diet.

Salmon is a major source of vital fish oils, and its many health benefits include protection against arthritis, heart disease, blood clots, stroke, high blood pressure, and high blood cholesterol. The EPA and DHA fatty acids it contains are linked with a reduced risk of depression and skin and breast cancer. They also help combat insulin resistance, which can be a precursor to diabetes, and help improve eczema and other inflammatory skin conditions. In addition, salmon contains a great range of the B vitamins—most of which are often in short supply on a gluten-free diet.

- Protection against cardiovascular diseases and stroke.
- Helps keep brain healthy and improves insulin resistance.
- Fish oils keep skin smooth, can help beat eczema, and prevent dry eyes.
- Helps minimize joint pain and arthritis and may reduce the risk of some cancers.

Practical tips:
For optimum omega-3 content, cook salmon lightly—poach or broil it. Frozen salmon retains the beneficial oils, vitamins, and minerals, but canned salmon loses a proportion of these nutrients. Hot- and cold-smoked salmon retain a good proportion of the omega-3 fats, but eat in moderation because the smoking process may increase the risk of cancer.

NUTRIENTS PER 3½ oz FRESH SALMON FILLET

Calories	183
Protein	19.9 g
Fat	10.8 g
EPA	0.69 g
DHA	1.29 g
Vitamin B6	0.64 mg
Vitamin B12	2.8 mcg
Folate	26 mcg
Niacin	7.5 mg
Vitamin C	3.9 mg
Vitamin E	1.9 mg
Magnesium	28 mg
Potassium	362 mg
Selenium	36.5 mcg
Zinc	0.4 mg

Salmon strips with potato wedges

SERVES 4   (v) (p)

1 cup fine cornmeal
1 teaspoon paprika
1 pound salmon fillet, skinned
    and sliced into
    12 chunky strips
1 egg, beaten
sunflower oil, for frying

Potato wedges

4 russet potatoes, cut into
    thick wedges
1–2 tablespoons olive oil
½ teaspoon paprika
salt, to taste

Method

1 Preheat the oven to 400°F. To make the wedges, dry the potato
  wedges on a clean dish towel. Spoon the oil into a roasting pan
  and put into the preheated oven briefly to heat. Add the potatoes
  to the pan and toss in the warm oil until well coated. Sprinkle with
  paprika and season with salt, then roast for 30 minutes, turning
  once, until crisp and golden.

2 Meanwhile, mix the cornmeal and paprika together on a plate. Dip
  each salmon strip into the beaten egg, then roll in the cornmeal
  mixture until evenly coated.

3 Heat enough oil to cover the bottom of a large, heavy skillet over
  medium heat. Carefully arrange half the salmon strips in the pan
  and cook for 6 minutes, turning halfway through, until golden. Drain
  on paper towels and keep warm while you cook the remaining
  salmon strips. Serve with the potato wedges.

94

TUNA

Another important source of heart-protecting omega-3 fats, fresh tuna is also rich in vitamin E, for healthy skin, and the B vitamins, especially B12, which are sometimes lacking in a gluten-free diet.

An excellent source of protein and especially rich in selenium and magnesium, a small 3½-ounce serving of tuna also contains around 20 percent of your daily vitamin E needs. The fish has a good content of EPA and DHA. DHA is particularly effective in keeping our hearts healthy and may also improve brain function and minimize depression. Eating tuna on a regular basis cuts death from heart disease by up to 50 percent—just one small 3½-ounce serving a week can provide the weekly recommended 1.4 g of these fats. Tuna is also a particularly good source of the B vitamins, with more than twice your RDA of vitamin B12 (vital for healthy blood and nerves) and half your niacin (which helps release energy from food).

- The protective fats found in tuna can cut heart disease deaths by up to 50 percent.
- High in protein.
- Rich in antioxidants selenium and magnesium for heart health.
- Rich in vitamin B12 and the range of B vitamins.

Practical tips:
Fresh or frozen tuna with its dense, meaty, flavorful flesh is an ideal choice of fish for nonfish lovers and is quick to cook. To retain all the health benefits of the omega-3 fats, cook for only a short time; cook a ¾-inch thick steak in a saucepan brushed with oil for 1–1½ minutes on each side. Or try adding sliced tuna to a stir-fry with sliced vegetables.

DID YOU KNOW?

Canned tuna contains much less omega-3 fat than fresh or frozen tuna and isn't classed as an oily fish at all.

NUTRIENTS PER 3½ oz FRESH TUNA FILLET

Calories	144
Protein	23 g
Fat	4.9 g
EPA	0.4 g
DHA	1.2 g
Vitamin B5	1 mg
Vitamin B6	0.5 mg
Vitamin B12	9.4 mcg
Niacin	8.3 mg
Vitamin E	1 mg
Iron	1 mg
Magnesium	50 mg
Potassium	252 mg
Selenium	36 mcg
Zinc	0.6 mg

Tuna steaks with Mediterranean butter

SERVES 4 (V) (P)

4 tuna steaks, each about
   1½ inches thick, at room
   temperature
olive oil, for brushing
salt and pepper, to taste
mixed salad greens, to serve

Mediterranean butter

1 garlic clove, finely chopped
1 stick butter, softened
2 tablespoons chopped fresh dill
4 black ripe olives, drained,
   pitted, and finely chopped
2 anchovy fillets in oil, drained
   and finely chopped
2 sun-dried tomatoes in oil,
   drained and finely chopped
finely grated zest of 1 lemon
pinch of cayenne pepper,
   or to taste
salt and pepper, to taste

Method

1 At least 3 hours before you plan to cook the tuna, make the butter. Put the garlic clove on a cutting board and sprinkle with salt. Use the flat side of a knife to crush and scrape the garlic until a paste forms. Beat together the garlic, butter, dill, olives, anchovies, sun-dried tomatoes, lemon zest, and cayenne pepper in a bowl until all the ingredients are mixed. Season with salt and pepper.

2 Scrape the butter mixture onto a piece of wax paper or plastic wrap and roll into a short log about 1 inch thick. Twist the ends of the paper to make a compact shape, then cut off any excess paper from one end. Stand the butter log upright in a glass and chill for at least 3 hours.

3 Heat a large, ridged grill pan over high heat. Brush the tuna with oil and season with salt and pepper on both sides. Place the tuna steaks in the pan and grill for 2 minutes. Brush the tuna with a little more oil, turn the steaks over, and continue cooking for 1 minute for medium-rare or up to 2½ minutes for well done. Transfer the tuna steaks to plates and top each with a slice of the chilled butter. Serve immediately with mixed salad greens.

95

TROUT

Trout has many of the benefits of salmon, but it is a lighter fish with less fat and more protein. It provides an excellent range of essential vitamins and minerals for the gluten-free diet.

Trout is classed as an oily fish and makes a good alternative to salmon if you find that too rich. Although trout contains fewer omega-3 fats (although is still a good source of these) and some of the B vitamins than salmon, it more than makes up for this by containing more vitamin B_{12} and more calcium, iron, magnesium, and zinc. Trout is extremely rich in potassium, a mineral that has several roles to play. It helps your heart beat properly and works with magnesium to help prevent an irregular heartbeat or palpitations. If you have high blood pressure, a weak heart, or heart rhythm problems, getting enough potassium is especially important—and eating a potassium-rich diet may lower your cholesterol, too.

- Contains heart-friendly omega-3 fats.
- High in potassium for a healthy heart.
- Good range of the B vitamins and minerals.
- Lowers cholesterol.

Practical tips:

The delicate flesh of trout needs only light cooking—try baking or broiling and serve with lemon wedges and salad. Alternatively, try steaming whole fish with Asian flavors, such as chile, ginger, garlic, and soy. Trout freezes well—freeze when as fresh as possible.

DID YOU KNOW?

Trout is a common freshwater fish found across the USA that is a popular choice for anglers.

NUTRIENTS PER 3½ oz FRESH TROUT FILLET

Calories	119
Protein	20.5 g
Fat	3.5 g
EPA	0.17 g
DHA	0.42 g
Vitamin B6	0.4 mg
Vitamin B12	4.5 mcg
Niacin	5.4 mg
Calcium	67 mg
Iron	0.7 mg
Magnesium	31 mg
Potassium	481 mg
Selenium	13 mcg
Zinc	1 mg

Trout terrine

SERVES 4　(v)　(P)

8 ounces trout fillets

6 ounces smoked trout,
　finely sliced

⅔ cup cream cheese

1 tablespoon crème fraîche,
　sour cream, or Greek yogurt

1 tablespoon horseradish sauce

grated zest of 1 lemon

2 tablespoons chopped fresh
　flat-leaf parsley

1 tablespoon snipped
　fresh chives

salt and pepper, to taste

salad greens, to serve

Method

1 Poach the trout fillets in a little water in a skillet for 3–4 minutes,
or until cooked. Drain well and let cool.

2 Line a small loaf pan with plastic wrap and then line with the slices
of smoked trout, leaving enough to overlap the top.

3 Skin and flake the trout fillets and mix together with the cream
cheese, crème fraîche, horseradish sauce, and lemon zest, and
season with salt and pepper.

4 Spoon a layer of the trout mixture into the lined pan. Sprinkle the
herbs over the trout mixture. Cover with the remaining trout mixture.
Fold over the smoked trout edges and cover with plastic wrap.
Press down and chill in the refrigerator for 2–3 hours.

5 Turn out of the pan and slice carefully, using a sharp knife. Serve
immediately garnished with salad greens.

96

CHEDDAR CHEESE

Hard cheeses, such as cheddar, have much to offer within a healthy gluten-free diet, because they pack in a high level of nutrients and are one of the foods richest in calcium.

DID YOU KNOW?

It takes around 2⅔ gallons of milk to make 2¼ pounds of cheddar. Mild cheddar is about three months old, whereas extra sharp, or vintage, cheddars are matured for around 18 months.

NUTRIENTS PER 1¾ oz CHEDDAR CHEESE

Calories	202
Protein	12.5 g
Fat	16.5 g
Vitamin A	150 mcg
Vitamin B$_2$	0.2 mg
Vitamin B$_{12}$	0.4 mcg
Vitamin D	0.3 mcg
Calcium	361 mg
Fluoride	17.9 mcg
Iodine	25 mcg
Magnesium	20 mg
Phosphorous	252 mg
Potassium	49 mg
Selenium	7 mcg
Zinc	1.5 mg

Cheddar cheese is rich in calcium—one 1¾-ounce serving provides more than one-third of your RDA. This mineral, along with magnesium also found in cheese, is essential for building and maintaining bone density and strength. Cheese also contains phosphorous, which binds with calcium to form bones and teeth; vitamin D, vital for bone formation; and arginine, which helps reduce tooth sensitivity. Calcium-rich foods speed up the metabolic rate, helping us to burn fat. The casein in cheese also helps boost metabolism, while the high protein and fat content keeps you feeling fuller for longer. Hard cheese is a good source of iodine, too, which helps the thyroid function, and vitamins B$_2$, B$_{12}$, and A, all of which may be in short supply on a gluten-free diet.

- High calcium content for healthy bones.
- Rich in minerals and compounds to keep teeth healthy.
- Helps speed up the metabolic rate and burn fat.
- One of the few good nonmeat sources of vitamin B$_{12}$.

Practical tips:

Hard cheese keeps best wrapped in wax paper and then stored in a container with airholes. It can also be frozen, whole or shredded. Add cheese to your diet by sprinkling it on soups, casseroles, and pasta dishes.

Zucchini and cheese gratin

SERVES 4–6 (V) (N)

4 tablespoons butter, plus extra
 for greasing
6 zucchini, sliced
2 tablespoons chopped fresh
 tarragon or a mixture of fresh
 mint, tarragon, and flat-leaf
 parsley
2 cups shredded cheddar
 cheese
½ cup milk
½ cup heavy cream
2 eggs, beaten
freshly grated nutmeg
salt and pepper, to taste

Method

1 Preheat the oven to 350°F.
 Grease a large ovenproof dish.

2 Melt the butter in a large skillet
 over medium–high heat. Add
 the zucchini and sauté for
 4–6 minutes, turning the
 slices over occasionally,
 until browned on both sides.
 Remove the zucchini from
 the skillet and drain on paper
 towels, then season with salt
 and pepper.

3 Spread half the zucchini over
 the bottom of the prepared
 dish. Sprinkle with half of
 the herbs and ¾ cup of the
 cheese. Repeat these layers
 once again.

4 Mix the milk, cream, and
 eggs together in a small bowl,
 and add nutmeg and season
 with salt and pepper. Pour
 this liquid over the zucchini,
 then sprinkle the top with the
 remaining cheese.

5 Bake in the preheated oven
 for 35–45 minutes, or until it is
 set in the center and golden
 brown. Remove from the oven
 and let stand for 5 minutes
 before serving straight from
 the dish.

97

GOAT CHEESE

Goat cheese has an unusual composition for a dairy product, being high in probiotics and low in lactose, and is a great cheese for anyone with digestive problems.

Goat milk cheese contains types of fatty acids that are similar to human milk and easier for the body to process than other milks. It is also easier to digest because the fat globules it contains are smaller than those in cow milk. The cheese is rich in probiotics—bacteria that can help the digestion process and may ease mild stomach problems. Relatively low in lactose, goat cheese is often suitable for people who are mildly lactose intolerant. A serving provides a similar vitamin and mineral content to hard cheeses and is a good source of vitamin A, phosphorus, niacin, and vitamin B_1. It is also high in calcium, which is not only vital for bone development and maintenance but also has a fat-burning effect for weight control.

- Fat types found in goat cheese are easily digestible.
- Rich in probiotics for digestive tract health.
- Good source of range of vitamins and minerals.
- High calcium content for bone health and weight control.

Practical tips:
Delicious eaten cold on gluten-free, whole-grain crackers or toast, goat cheese is also great to use as a melted cheese topping in a variety of recipes. It goes well with beets, onions, apples, celery, and grapes.

DID YOU KNOW?

It takes around more than 1¼ gallons of milk to make 1 pound of goat cheese, and it is one of the earliest dairy foods known to have been produced.

NUTRIENTS PER 1¾ oz GOAT CHEESE

Calories	182
Protein	10.8 g
Fat	15 g
Vitamin A	220 mcg
Vitamin B_2	0.3 mg
Vitamin B_3	0.6 mg
Vitamin D	0.3 mcg
Calcium	149 mg
Magnesium	15 mg
Phosphorous	188 mg
Potassium	79 mg
Zinc	0.3 mg

Lentil and goat cheese tomatoes

SERVES 4   (F) (V) (D) (N)

¼ cup dried green lentils
4 beefsteak tomatoes
1 tablespoon olive oil
2 large shallots, finely chopped
1 garlic clove, crushed
1 tablespoon chopped
   fresh thyme
4 ounces hard goat cheese,
   diced
salt and pepper, to taste
mixed salad, to serve

Method

1 Bring a small saucepan of water to a boil over medium–high heat. Add the lentils, return to a boil, and cook for 20–25 minutes, or until tender. Drain well.

2 Meanwhile, preheat the oven to 400°F. Cut a slice from the tops of the tomatoes and set aside. Scoop out the pulp from the center and coarsely chop.

3 Heat the oil in a skillet over medium heat and sauté the shallots, stirring, for 3–4 minutes to soften. Add the garlic and chopped tomato pulp and cook for an additional 3–4 minutes, or until any excess liquid has evaporated.

4 Put the tomatoes into a shallow baking dish. Stir the lentils and thyme into the skillet, and season with salt and pepper. Stir in the goat cheese and then spoon the mixture into the tomatoes.

5 Place the lids on the tomatoes and bake in the preheated oven for 15–20 minutes, or until tender. Serve immediately with mixed salad.

98

EGGS

Eggs contain almost the whole range of nutrients that can be lacking on a gluten-free diet and have several additional health benefits.

NUTRIENTS PER LARGE EGG

Calories	80
Protein	7 g
Fat	5.3 g
Vitamin A	91 mcg
Vitamin B₂	0.3 mg
Vitamin B₁₂	0.5 mcg
Choline	141 mg
Folate	26 mcg
Vitamin D	11.5 mcg
Vitamin E	0.6 mg
Calcium	31 mg
Phosphorous	111 mg
Potassium	77 mg
Zinc	0.7 mg

Eggs from hens provide the whole range of essential amino acids that make up a complete protein and so are especially useful in a vegetarian diet. They are high in most of the major vitamins, including A, B_2, B_{12}, D, and E, and minerals, including calcium, zinc, and phosphorous. It can be hard to get adequate amounts of all these nutrients on a gluten-free diet. Eggs are particularly high in the B vitamin choline, which helps prevent high levels of harmful homocysteine (linked to cardiovascular disease and osteoporosis) in the blood. Eggs from hens allowed to eat a natural, pasture/woodland diet are a good source of heart-friendly omega-3 fats, but even other types of eggs have been shown to raise "good" HDL cholesterol.

• Excellent source of complete protein.
• High in many vitamins and minerals.
• High in choline for heart health.
• Can help raise HDL cholesterol.

Practical tips:
Store eggs in the refrigerator or at cool room temperature—let warm slightly in the kitchen before boiling in their shells or the shells may crack. If using several eggs in a recipe, first break each one separately into a bowl to check the egg looks fresh (rounded yolk, cloudy white, no odor).

Angel food cake

SERVES 8   Ⓒ

butter, for greasing
10 egg whites
⅓ cup white rice flour
½ cup tapioca (cassava) flour
½ cup cornstarch
½ cup potato flour
1½ cups superfine sugar
   or granulated sugar
1½ teaspoons cream of tartar
½ teaspoon vanilla extract
½ teaspoon salt
confectioners' sugar, for dusting

Method

1 Preheat the oven to 350°F. Grease an 8-inch round cake pan and line it with parchment paper.

2 Let the egg whites sit for about 30 minutes at room temperature in a large bowl. Sift the white rice flour, tapioca flour, cornstarch, potato flour, and ¾ cup plus 2 tablespoons of the sugar into a separate bowl.

3 Whisk together the egg whites with the cream of tartar, vanilla extract, and salt until soft peaks form. Gradually add the remaining sugar until stiff peaks develop. Add the flour mixture and fold in carefully to combine.

4 Spoon the batter into the prepared pan and bake in the preheated oven for about 45 minutes, until firm to the touch and a toothpick inserted in the center comes out clean.

5 Remove from the oven and, leaving the cake in the pan, turn upside down to cool on a wire rack. Once cool, remove from the pan and dust with confectioners' sugar.

99

MILK

Rich in calcium and several other nutrients that a gluten-free diet can often lack, milk is worth including in your diet every day.

The amount of nutrients milk contains means it is really more of a food than a drink. One-quarter of the calories in a serving of just under 8 fluid ounces come from protein and around one-third from fat—both help keep hunger pangs at bay, so milk is an ideal snack. This amount will also contain around one-third of your RDA of calcium (which can be low on a gluten-free diet), all of your RDA of vitamin B_{12}, and one-quarter of your RDA of vitamin B_2—a vitamin that helps release the energy from both protein and fat in your body. Milk is a good source of choline (a lesser-known B vitamin that protects against cardiovascular disease, osteoporosis, and arthritis) and vitamin A for healthy eyes and skin.

- Good source of calcium to maintain and repair bones and to help prevent osteoporosis.
- Contains most of the B vitamins.
- High level of vitamin A.
- Choline content protects against heart disease and arthritis.

Practical tips:
Store milk in the refrigerator to retain the B vitamins and keep well-sealed so that it doesn't absorb aromas from other foods in the refrigerator. Make a healthy, potassium-rich milk shake by blending milk with a banana. A glass of milk before bedtime really can help you sleep, because the tryptophan it contains will boost brain serotonin and aid relaxation.

DID YOU KNOW?

Organic and/or grass-fed cow milk is a good source of omega-3 fats, as well as a variety of antioxidant compounds and vitamin E. The milk from penned animals fed on grain-base feed is not as rich in these nutrients.

NUTRIENTS PER 1 CUP/7 FL OZ LOW-FAT (2% FAT) MILK

Calories	100
Protein	6.6 g
Fat	4 g
Carbohydrate	9.6 g
Vitamin A	61.2 mcg
Vitamin B_2	0.4 mg
Vitamin B_5	0.7 mg
Vitamin B_{12}	1 mcg
Choline	32.8 mg
Calcium	240 mg
Magnesium	22 mg
Potassium	280 mg
Zinc	1 mg

Crème caramel

SERVES 4 Ⓥ Ⓝ

butter, for greasing
1 cup sugar
¼ cup water
½ lemon
2 cups milk
1 vanilla bean
2 extra-large eggs
2 extra-large egg yolks

Method

1 Preheat the oven to 325°F. Lightly grease the bottom and sides of four ramekins (individual ceramic dishes). To make the caramel, put ⅓ cup of the sugar with the water in a saucepan over medium–high heat and cook, stirring, until the sugar dissolves. Boil until the syrup turns a deep golden brown, then immediately remove from the heat and squeeze in a few drops of lemon juice. Divide evenly among the ramekins, swirl around to line the bottom, and set aside.

2 Pour the milk into a saucepan. Slit the vanilla bean lengthwise and add it to the milk. Bring to a boil, remove the saucepan from the heat, and stir in the remaining sugar, stirring until it dissolves. Keep to one side.

3 Beat together the eggs and egg yolks in a bowl. Pour the milk mixture over them, whisking. Remove the vanilla bean. Strain the egg mixture into a bowl, then divide evenly among the ramekins.

4 Place the dishes in a roasting pan. Boil some water and carefully pour the hot water into the pan so that it comes two-thirds of the way up the sides of the dishes.

5 Bake in the preheated oven for 1–1¼ hours, or until the tip of a knife inserted in the center comes out clean. Let cool completely. Cover with plastic wrap and let chill for at least 24 hours.

6 Run a blunt knife around the edge of each dish. Place an upturned serving plate, with a rim, on top of each dish, then invert the plate and dish, giving a sharp shake halfway over. Lift off the ramekin dishes and serve.

100 YOGURT

One of the healthiest dairy foods to include in a gluten-free diet, regular plain yogurt with live, or "bio," cultures has a special role in maintaining digestive tract health.

Yogurt has long been eaten for its health-giving properties. Yogurt with live cultures, which contains billions of bacteria, such as acidophilus and bifidobacteria, is a valuable digestive aid. These "friendly" bacteria line the digestive tract, protect the digestive system from harm, help to relieve bloating and constipation, and boost the immune system. Yogurt also has many of the health benefits of cheese, being high in calcium for bone health and aiding relaxation and sleep. For those watching their weight, yogurt can even boost fat loss, particularly around the waist. Yogurt with live cultures may also lower LDL cholesterol and raise HDL.

- Helps keep the digestive system healthy and regular.
- Boosts the immune system.
- High calcium content for bone health and relaxation.
- Burns abdominal fat and improves blood cholesterol profile.

Practical tips:
Yogurt can be made with cow, goat, sheep, or buffalo milk, but cow milk yogurt is the most common. Yogurt, fruit, and whole-grain cereal is one of the healthiest breakfasts you can eat. Also try stirring plain yogurt into soups, casseroles, and sauces, or use as a topping for dessert instead of cream. Bring the yogurt to room temperature before adding to hot dishes to help prevent it from curdling.

DID YOU KNOW?

Yogurt got its name from the Turkish word *yogurur*, which means "long life," and it has been consumed throughout Turkey and the Middle East for more than 5,000 years.

NUTRIENTS PER ½ CUP/3½ OZ REGULAR YOGURT WITH LIVE CULTURES

Calories	61
Protein	3.5 g
Fat	3.2 g
Carbohydrate	4.7 g
Vitamin A	30 mcg
Vitamin B5	0.4 mg
Vitamin B12	0.4 mcg
Calcium	121 mg
Iodine	35 mcg
Fluoride	12 mcg
Magnesium	12 mg
Phosphorous	95 mg
Potassium	155 mg
Zinc	0.6 mg

Frozen yogurt cups

MAKES 12 (V) (D)

2 cups low-fat plain yogurt

1½ tablespoons finely grated
    orange zest

2 cups mixed berries, such as
    blueberries, raspberries, and
    hulled strawberries, plus
    extra to decorate

fresh mint sprigs, to decorate
    (optional)

Method

1 Set the freezer to rapid freeze 2 hours before freezing this dish, if it
   has this setting. Line a 12-section muffin pan with 12 muffin cups,
   or use ramekins (individual ceramic dishes) on a baking sheet.

2 Mix together the yogurt and orange zest in a large bowl. Cut any
   large strawberries into pieces so that they are the same size as the
   blueberries and raspberries.

3 Add the fruit to the yogurt, then spoon into the muffin cups or
   ramekins. Freeze for 2 hours, or until just frozen. Decorate with
   extra fruit and mint sprigs, if using, and serve. Remember to return
   the freezer to its original setting afterward.

INDEX